# Living the
# Internet Lifestyle

# Other Titles By Connie Ragen Green

The Weekend Marketer: Say Goodbye to the '9 to 5', Build an Online Business, and Live the Life You Love

Time Management Strategies for Entrepreneurs: How to Manage Your Time to Increase Your Bottom Line

The Inner Game of Internet Marketing

Membership Sites Made Simple: Start Your Own Membership Site for Passive Online Income

Article Marketing: How to Attract New Prospects, Create Products, and Increase Your Income

Targeted Traffic Techniques for Affiliate Marketers

Huge Profits With Affiliate Marketing: How to Build an Online Empire by Recommending What You Love

Huge Profits with a Tiny List: 50 Ways to use Relationship Marketing to Increase Your Bottom Line

# Living the Internet Lifestyle

## Quit Your Job, Become an Entrepreneur, and Live Your Ideal Life

By
Connie Ragen Green

*Copyright © 2013 by Hunter's Moon Publishing*

*978-1-937988-08-1*

 Hunter's Moon Publishing

*Photography by Tony Laidig*
*Cover design by Shawn Hansen*

# Dedication

This book is dedicated to two people who have made this last year a memorable one for me. Without them my online life would neither be as sweet and fulfilling as it is today, nor as prosperous and joyful.

Nicole Dean is a special person in my life. She has known me for about five years, first as a complete newbie emailing her with my questions, later as an affiliate, and now as a friend and colleague. Nicole is wicked smart, but always makes me feel like I can achieve anything I set my mind to doing. Nicole, I am proud to call you my friend.

The other is Dennis Becker, a man for whom I have the greatest respect and hold in the highest esteem. I have learned so much from him during the three short years we have been friends and colleagues. Dennis has a way of being a good listener when you need to talk, sharing brilliant marketing tips when you least expect it, and making you feel like what you want to achieve is worthwhile. Dennis, I appreciate you.

# Table of Contents

# Foreword

I'm thrilled that Connie Ragen Green has asked me to write a foreword for this book. I've been a fan and a friend of hers since around 2010, and consider it an honor to contribute here.

Living the Internet marketing lifestyle... what is it, and what does it mean to me?

I'd have to preface that answer with telling a little about myself. I'm an early baby boomer, and was raised in relative poverty. My parents and grandparents worked very hard to scrape by, and we did without a lot of things that are taken for granted today.

One of the things that we learned was that it was expected that we'd go to school, graduate from high school, and then hopefully go on to college and eventually land a well paying job with a large and established company.

I did that, and enjoyed it, until I was 33 years old with a wife, toddler and teenaged stepson. Then the entrepreneurial bug hit me like a ton of bricks.

I wanted more for myself and my family, so I started my own software consulting company, which I gave up for the retail store experience 8 years later, which led to finding a spot online.

Along the way, during the retail store days, I accumulated unfathomable (well over 6-figures of) debt. The stress was more than I could bear and started affecting my health.

Something was terribly wrong, and I had to do something about it.

In 2005, after trying and failing at too many things to count, I started succeeding online, and after writing my first book in 2006 about a simple but never before discussed strategy, found a way to leverage that small amount of fame into much more.

Now I'm writing in 2013 with the debt gone, and a lifestyle that I couldn't even begin to imagine in the earlier years.

I know that you've probably seen the IM guru sales pages where they show their huge homes, their fancy cars, their boats, their gadgets, their jewelry, along with their overstuffed (and Photoshopped in some cases) PayPal account balances... that's not me.

I still drive a minivan that's seen its best days (2000 model), live in the same house that I bought in 1978, and my clothes... well let me say that I probably embarrass my son when we're seen together.

Things aren't lifestyle.

Now I have freedom. Freedom to wake up at whatever time I want (usually early but by choice), work as many or as few hours as I want, take off whenever I choose, and do things I enjoy, not what I'm told to do.

For example... I grew up in northwestern Pennsylvania, where snow falls from around October through April or May and in abundance. So when I first experienced a vacation at the oceanfront I absolutely fell in love with the experience.

My first time was when I was in the Army, I guess around 1969 or so, at Virginia Beach, Virginia, near where I was stationed.

Since then my dream has always been to live on the ocean, and last year I decided that I wanted to find out what a condo would cost on the boardwalk in Atlantic City (home of the famous Monopoly streets, remember?).

I found one that my wife and I liked, but when I tried to get a mortgage, the bank turned us down because of a problem with the building that they didn't like. So we lost that one, and were very disappointed.

Since I was working for myself, I determined that the next time I found a place I liked, I would be able to make an offer without applying for a mortgage, and barely 4 months later, a steal of a deal, combined with a bigger than expected tax refund, combined with a real estate agent that confided that the seller was really wanting to move, and we had our vacation home on the ocean, fully furnished and ready to move in.

Now I can visit there any time I want, breath the sea air, and take long walks on the boardwalk at sunrise... pure heaven to me.

Freedom. Freedom that would not be possible if I worked for someone else. Freedom that eludes probably 95% of the population. Freedom to work on my business projects from my homes or my office, whichever I choose.

Now that doesn't mean that I can quit working on my business, nor would I want to, because my business is something that I love.

So further freedom is that I can work on my business projects from either of my homes or my office, whichever I choose.

I get the opportunity to help people, make lots of online friends in many, many countries, and more than anything provide products and services that truly make a difference in their businesses and their lives.

My fondest wish is that people that I touch will some day, if they want to, be able to live the lifestyle that I enjoy...

... or if they prefer, they can buy the fancy homes or cars or jewelry or gadgets or vacations.

When I was a boy there was no such thing as a computer other than in the military and government. When I took my first job, there was no Internet, nor even such a thing as a personal computer. When I established my retail store, there was no World Wide Web, and certainly no Google or Amazon. When I first came online as a fledgling IM'er (first with eBay) there was no Twitter, no Facebook, no YouTube, and I guess no smart phones.

My granddaughter (now 18 months old) will probably believe that as easily as my son believes that I walked to school through 2 feet of snow, uphill, every day, and lived without so much as cable television.

All true.

Now we have that and so much more, but more than anything we have opportunity galore.

We live in such amazing times now, and who knows what it will be like 5 years from now when future readers are reading these words?

What do you want to do? Where do you want to live? Who do you want to inspire? What kind of legacy do you want to leave behind?

I'm thrilled with my lifestyle, it has all been made possible because I started marketing products online, and decided to help others do the same.

I hope you enjoy Connie's book, and I hope that you're inspired to seek the lifestyle that you deserve.

Dennis Becker
Earn1KaDay.net
June 4, 2013

# Preface

*'Do what others won't, for a year;*
*Live the way others cannot, forever.'*

Having written eight books during the past three years I am keenly aware of the fact that no more should be written by me unless I truly have something to say on the topic of online marketing as an entrepreneur. With that being said, I believe that the message I am imparting in this book may in fact be the most important one I am sharing so far in my career as an online marketing strategist and entrepreneur.

We've just lived through the worst recession since the Great Depression. Not one of us can say we were not affected by this, whether it was up close and personal or through a close friend, neighbor, or family member. Jobs were lost, careers were thwarted, homes were foreclosed upon, and families displaced. Even pets were affected when people so desperate to care for their children were sometimes forced to make the hard decision to leave their furry friends behind. The government cannot be expected to put everything back the way it was in the past; our futures depend upon us taking action and moving forward. It's about taking personal responsibility for your life and your world. Doing so will change your own life, the lives of your family members and friends, and the lives of people you may never get the chance to meet.

The intention of this book is to share my own experiences, as well as those of my students, in a way that will make clear the importance of becoming an entrepreneur in order to live the life you choose. I believe we all learn best by example, and with that in mind I will share the intimate details of what it takes to be successful, both personally and professionally.

I truly believe that at the end of the day we all want the same thing from our life; work that is meaningful and satisfying, relationships that are fulfilling and rewarding, and a spiritual connection to let us know that it's about more than us. The information I am sharing here will bring you closer to this end.

It will then be up to you to read this book, filing away what resonates with you and discarding the rest. At the end, when you have your own self-imposed marching orders, move forward without haste and enjoy what is to take place in your own life that will change you forever.

I'll also be sharing what the Internet lifestyle looks like, so that you can better imagine how you would change your life if your income and free time became more abundant during this next year. It takes hard work, dedication, and perseverance, and that's why most people will never achieve their goals. You will be different because you now have access to this detailed, step by step training on what to do today to begin your journey as an online entrepreneur.

My motto has always been 'If I can do it, you can do it' and this has helped people around the world to change their lives.

Connie Ragen Green
June 21, 2013

# Introduction

I'm writing this from the front porch of my house in Santa Barbara, California on a clear day in December. I've just returned from a speaking engagement in London, and in a few days I'm headed down to Central America to spend a week with friends and family members to celebrate the holidays. This would not be of major importance or great significance except for the fact that I am now living the lifestyle I had previously only dreamed of, and it all started when I made the decision to escape from my day jobs, change my mindset, work on my 'Inner Game', and to come online to build a business as an entrepreneur back at the end of 2005.

As a young child growing up in Los Angeles, California and, later, in Miami, Florida we were extremely poor. It was just my mother and I, and we never had a car or a telephone or anything else the other families around us all seemed to have. At age twelve I began working, first by mowing lawns and babysitting, and then by working as a waitress in the local coffee shops. I did manage to go to college, but even then I felt out of place with the other students. My mindset was one of poverty, even though I would not have believed or understood that at the time. Where others saw hope and opportunity, I saw challenges and struggle. After graduating from college I wandered through my 20s in a variety of jobs – claims adjuster for an insurance company, bank teller, manager of a coin laundry, and then as a real estate agent.

It was while working in real estate that I finally began to view my life a little bit differently. Perhaps it was the influence of the people I was working with, or the small successes I was beginning to experience in my work as a broker, but I found myself wanting more out of life than what I was getting at that time and believed that this was indeed possible. It was also during this time that I began to experience some financial success.

I could see the direct correlation between some of the activities I was engaging in and the closed deals that resulted in large commission checks for me. It felt good to finally be earning more money than I had ever made in the past. The only problem was that I was not engaging in any of these activities consistently enough to be able to identify specific actions that were both rewarding and lucrative. The pieces of the puzzle were not coming together completely for me at that time, but the seed of what might be possible had been planted in my mind.

In January of 1986 I had just arrived at the real estate office where I was working at the time to find everyone huddled around a small television set to see the launch of the Space Shuttle. As I got close enough to see the screen a hush fell over the room. The Challenger had broken apart and disintegrated before our eyes. This was the first time a teacher had been aboard this type of space mission, and this immediately made me think back to when I was younger and had wanted to become a teacher myself. I made a conscious decision at that moment to pursue my dream of becoming a classroom teacher, and within nine months I was teaching in a classroom while completing my credential.

This marked the very first time I had taken action in such a dramatically focused way. Perhaps it was the emotional tone of what had happened to Christa McAuliffe, the teacher aboard the space craft, and the others that drove me to follow through with something I was so very passionate about. I had wanted to become a teacher for so many years, but had never taken the necessary steps to meet my goal. I had never even discussed this dream with anyone because I thought it would never come true. This time was different, and it felt good to finally be achieving my dreams and having control over my life and my destiny.

Over the next twenty years I worked as a classroom teacher, serving students in Kindergarten through high school. I even taught some adult school night classes for a couple of years. My favorite grade to teach was fifth grade. The kids at that age were so responsive to an adult role model, and it was a joy to watch them grow and learn. During my first few years of teaching I was able to share my own experiences, interests, and knowledge with the kids each year as part of our learning environment; over time this was eliminated and I could only teach the prescribed course of study. I came to understand that the public schools in America were designed to produce a constant stream of obedient and compliant workers for the corporate and manufacturing sectors of our country. My dream was to teach the creative leaders of tomorrow, not to train young people into submission. One day in the spring of 2005, after a disturbing conversation with a group of school administrators, I came to the conclusion that I would leave teaching in the next year or two and pursue a different path for the next phase of my life.

I am also a three time cancer survivor, and going through those experiences made me realize that I needed a way to make a living that did not require me to be gone from home twelve to fourteen hours each day, six or seven days each week.

This left me in quite a conundrum as I had to decide what I really wanted out of my life. If you have had this experience in your own life then you may already know what I'm talking about here. It's a complicated process to go from where you are in your life at this specific moment in time to an entirely new way of acting, believing, and interacting with others. You must choose to either go on with the life you currently have and be content with whatever might happen, or to be willing to move way out of your comfort zone and be responsible for what you really want to experience during the remainder of your life by playing bigger than you've ever thought possible. I was ready for a huge change in my life, so I took a leap of faith and dug in with both heels.

Over the course of the next several months I began to read everything I could get my hands on to find out who I was, what I cared about, and which direction I wanted to take my life. It was as if my eyes were wide open for the first time in ages, and I was intoxicated at the possibilities that appeared and unfolded before me. I knew then that I could determine the outcome of my life and that any decisions I made would either move me closer to or further away from my dreams. My previous life had been dominated by fear, and now I could see why that was so unnecessary. I was afraid of not having enough money, of being judged by others, of making the wrong decisions in my daily life, of losing my job, of not having friends, and of so much more. Now I was starting to turn that around into a positive approach to my life, where fears could easily be overcome and hope was definitely within reach.

That summer of 2005 I turned fifty years old, and I felt as though I had the rest of my life in front of me in a way I hadn't felt since I was a young child. That's when I began writing down my thoughts in a journal, and also drawing some simple pictures. I've never been much of an artist, but suddenly I wanted to draw meaningful pictures to express my thoughts and ideas for my future. I bought a pad of drawing paper and some colored pencils and began to sketch. I ended up creating a picture of myself sitting at a desk, looking out the window and having my dogs playing on the floor beside me. The windows were covered with white plantation shutters, something I had never had anywhere I had lived. The view out the window was of the hills and canyons that are familiar in southern California. I knew people with this type of view, but had never had one myself.

Within eight months that picture became my reality. I moved from the house I had lived in for the previous fourteen years into a brand new home in a new city, Santa Clarita, which was twenty-five miles away. When friends came to see the new house and I showed them the picture I had drawn, none of them could believe it had been drawn before the new house was even built. My office, on the second floor, looks out past the white plantation shutters on to the canyons as far as the eye can see. My dogs love playing while I am busy at my computer doing this business that I love.

I was now in control of my future and I began to see things very differently. I realized that I had to take full and complete responsibility for everything that happened in my life, whether it was positive or negative. I reflected on situations in my past and saw that my perception of what had occurred was very different, in many cases, from what was actually going on at that time.

At this point I was ready to jump in and start a business on the Internet as an online entrepreneur. My 'Inner Game', which I consider to be more important than business training or experience, was coming together in a way that made me feel excited and confident in my ability to be successful. I was surrounding myself with positive, upbeat people, as well as spending time each day studying what I needed to learn in order to launch my business in a way that would skyrocket my success quickly. Nothing could stop me now because I had a different outlook on life and was determined to see it through.

This was at the end of 2005, and on through 2006 I set about the task of laying a solid foundation for my business. This included starting to blog at least twice a week, writing articles to submit to the article directories, attending and then hosting teleseminars on my topic, learning more about affiliate marketing, and connecting with others who were doing something similar on the Internet. You must remember that this was before social media, so connecting with others took some creative thinking and implementing. These activities became something I named 'The 5 Pronged Approach™' and I'll be discussing it in more detail later on in this book. Also, I did not have my own product to sell until the end of 2006, so recommending other people's products as an affiliate made the most sense for me. These are all tactics, so now it was time to focus on the strategies that would work so that I could replace my previous income and work exclusively online.

'Inner Game' strategies were the first ones I worked on, because I knew by now that if I had my thinking in order making money and achieving my goals would never be an issue for me again during my lifetime. That was a powerful thought and quite a revelation for me at that time, but after spending several months in a positive state of mind I was confident enough to believe in myself in a way I had never been able to in the past. I used to stand in front of my bathroom mirror and tell myself that I was smart and dedicated and could achieve any goals I wanted to achieve. Then I would sit down at my computer and write for at least thirty minutes.

This writing was therapeutic in that I was writing about many experiences that had not been very pleasant in my life, and then reframing them in a way that served me better than to just complain and feel like a victim. For example, I wrote about the school principal who had been so unkind to me over the years and reframed that into her seeing the special qualities I possessed and wanting to help me to improve upon them. This was a way of forgiving, accepting, and having gratitude and appreciation for people I had known over the years.

Writing was also a way for me to hone my skills by getting as much practice as possible. If you are familiar with the concept of the 'Ten Thousand Hours Rule', which states that success in any area of life is a matter of practicing a specific task for at least 10,000 hours, you will see how powerful this concept can be. I thought back to my early days of teaching in the classroom and realized that everything came easier once I had been at it for four to five years, which equates to about ten thousand hours of actual teaching. I had always wanted to become a writer, so putting in my time in this area seemed like the wisest step for me to take to achieve my goal.

And so I continued to write, learn, and create as my business grew, and within about eighteen months I had replaced my previous income and was now surpassing it. It felt wonderful to finally be in a position to help others build their businesses and to become a teacher once again. Along the way I have connected with so many people that I otherwise would never had met, and some of these people I now count as my dearest friends and business associates. I travel the world for both business and pleasure and meet people on the other side of the planet that are pursuing goals in their lives that are very similar to mine. It's true that we all share much more in common than we have differences. Working online makes all of this possible in my life.

So, to kind of sum up what I have just shared I will say that I had a 'change of attitude' during 2005, when it became clear to me that my views were so different from those of the school district, and also when I came to the realization that I wanted to work from home. It would take almost a year for me to experience a 'change in behavior'. This combination of actions, the start of which occurs in your mind when you have a moment of clarity about your present situation, and goes on to become a shift in your thinking and daily activities is what your life's journey is all about.

I have run my business from my home offices in southern California, as well as from the beach in Santa Barbara; from Internet cafés in downtown Amsterdam and in rural China; the convention center in Bangkok, Thailand; my family's summer cottage in Finland; a pub in London, and from spots all over the United States where I can easily get an Internet signal through a WiFi connection. Being able to travel extensively is a part of the life I have created for myself, and it is so much sweeter when I can bring my business along for the ride.

I won't say that the fears and lack of confidence from my previous life are forever behind me; every once in awhile I hear those little voices telling me I'm not smart enough and don't deserve the success I'm now enjoying.

When this happens I simply make a list of what I am most grateful for in my life, along with a list of my accomplishments over the past few years, to know that I am on the right path for what I want from my life on a daily basis.

The life of an online entrepreneur suits my new lifestyle quite well, and I would encourage you to explore this way of life if it resonates with you. It allows me to continue to be a teacher; something that I thought was gone forever when I left the classroom. It has also given me the gift of creativity, and I had not thought of myself in this way at any time previously during the course of my lifetime. Teaching and creating are excellent ways to make a living while also helping others and feeling good about what you're doing each day for the ultimate experience in a rewarding business.

The best advice I have for you is to always keep it simple. People come to me all the time with overcomplicated, complex business plans that make my eyes glaze over. None of these ever come to fruition, reinforcing my beliefs about the importance of simplicity in our lives and our businesses. Simple, direct goals where you take action and implement what you're learning will always work best in life.

Throughout this book I will reference many stories about getting your 'Inner Game' into synch with who you are and how you function and appear to the outside world.

These are the gems that will take you to the next level in your life and in your online business to help you become a successful entrepreneur. You will want to write them now and refer to them regularly as you move forward.

So, you may be wondering how your 'Inner Game' comes into play with my online business advice. The answer is that you must continue to believe in yourself and have confidence each day as you go through the different prongs and apply them to your business. No amount of training, or of knowing the specific winning tactics and strategies for business will make a difference unless you know who you are and what you wish to achieve. This is crucial to being able to attract money and opportunities from anywhere you are and whatever you are involved with in your life.

Write down your goals and then take action each and every day to move closer to achieving them. Connect with the people who are already living the lifestyle that resonates with you and learn more about how they made significant changes in their lives over time. Ask questions, seek out knowledge, and then move forward. Know that you can be, do, or have anything you want in your life simply by making the conscious decision and positive choice to take massive, inspired actions towards your goals.

What you have to share matters to others, and no one can deliver your message in the same way that you will be able to do it. This is the time to simplify, collaborate, and move forward as an online entrepreneur, so incorporate this new way of thinking into your daily thinking and see what's possible in your own life experience.

# Section One

# Why Would You Want This Lifestyle?

At some point along the way I made the decision to dedicate my life to serving others. This was not a conscious decision at first, as my life had had many ups and downs along the way, as many other people have had as well. My focus initially was on just doing what needed to be done to stay afloat in my own day to day life.

Being of service to others became more important to me during the 1980s when I got involved in three situations that changed my perspective. I became a foster parent to a Kindergartner who had an alcoholic mother and crack addicted father, served as a Big Sister to a mentally retarded African-American girl who had been abandoned on a bus bench on the night she was born, and began going door to door to collect canned goods for the local food pantry one Saturday each month. It was then that I realized the world needed more people to serve in any way possible, and that even by doing something small for one other human being you were making a positive difference in the world.

By the year 2000 this idea had become more of a conscious choice as I began to dream about being able to have more time and money to help more people. In 2005 my feelings came to a head as I made the difficult decision to resign from my job as a classroom teacher at age fifty and seek out the life of an online entrepreneur. I had no idea how this would become my reality, but I was willing to take a leap of faith that it could be achieved in a timely manner that would help me to accomplish not only my financial goals at the time, but also my life's goals as well.

I will now make the assumption that if the title of this book caught your eye, or if it was recommended to you and if you're still reading this far in, then you must have at least a curious interest in finding out why someone would choose to live the Internet lifestyle. Because this entails leaving a traditional working life behind, with all of its expectations and requirements, then you must have at least a passing interest in seeing the value of living your life this way.

Over my lifetime, including the more than thirty years I worked with and for other people, I always dreamed of having more flexibility in my daily schedule. During my twenty years as a classroom teacher in Los Angeles, I would look longingly out the window and wish I could spend more time outside. During my vacation times from school, while I was working every day as a real estate broker and residential appraiser, at times driving up to three hundred miles in a single day, I would look out the car window and wish I could be at the beach or at the movies, or at any of a dozen other places.

It wasn't that I was unhappy working as a teacher or in real estate, I was just exhausted and desiring of another lifestyle that would afford me both the time and the money to pursue other things in my life. I loved teaching for many years, and appreciated the opportunity to earn additional income with real estate, but I longed for a life where I would have more of a chance to travel and to do volunteer work to help others in need. It was time freedom and financial freedom I was seeking in my life.

Because I did not have that life myself and had no friends or acquaintances who did, I could only imagine what it would be like for me to experience it firsthand. Knowing what I now do, it would have been an excellent idea for me to volunteer at a charity event to meet new people and to get more of an idea of what it really was that I wanted to do. By putting yourself in front of the life you are dreaming of you are more easily able to visualize what that life could look like for you.

It never occurred to me that I could live the life of my dreams by operating a business exclusively from a laptop computer. It wasn't until the fall of 2005, after listening to some CDs about setting up niche websites to earn money from selling information products that I realized this life was truly a possibility for me. Tens of thousands of people around the world enjoy this lifestyle to one degree or another, and I was ready to come aboard. Even though I had no idea where to begin I made the conscious decision to get started right away. My initial goal was to learn as much as possible in the shortest amount of time so that I could put the pieces together. I was ready to take action to start my business and enter the next phase of my life. Working from home would make my life much easier, and I was open to what that could become in the future.

That was my big 'Reason Why' that led me to seeking out a life as an online entrepreneur. It turned out that I didn't really want to stay home every day and work at my computer, so I began travelling to live events around the United States and finally abroad. I enjoyed this immensely. These days my dreams are a reality as I travel the world, divide my time between homes in two incredible cities, and volunteer my time and donate my resources to organizations such as Rotary, an international service organization and Elk's, a group based in the United States that serves disabled children and veterans. My family has benefitted in many ways because life is so much easier for all of us as we are able to strive for and reach our full potential without having to focus each day primarily on maintaining the basic necessities of life.

# What Is The Internet Lifestyle?

What exactly does it mean to live the 'Internet lifestyle'? Now that I have been doing just that exclusively since 2006, I feel uniquely and unabashedly qualified to answer this question. I think of the Internet lifestyle as one in which my business is portable and simply an extension of who I am as a human being.

People who talk about 'getting away from it all' simply do not love what they do for a living enough to keep it close at hand. Can you imagine Kobe Bryant, forward and shooting guard for the Los Angeles Lakers basketball team, going on vacation with the intention of getting away from anything that would remind him of the game he loves? Imagine Bill Gates wanting to spend a few days without hearing about technology. Would that happen? Of course not. This would be ludicrous. Now that does not mean Kobe has a basketball in his hands 24/7 or that Bill is constantly in front of a computer or other device. People who love what they do are connected with it at a cellular level. Their mission is to serve others, and that requires a heartfelt commitment.

The Internet lifestyle has become my life, and I love every aspect of it. Every morning I spring out of bed with new ideas to implement, people with whom I wish to connect, books to read (and write!) and products and courses to create.

Lifestyle Design is the unofficial term that's been given to this type of living during the past decade, and you can think of it any way you choose. Some people describe it as early retirement, but I personally left the work force at age fifty and can't relate to that definition. Instead, I think of the Internet lifestyle as one in which you make your own hours, do what suits you each day, and serve the people you have always wanted to help. It fits in with the subtitle of this book, which is to quit your job, become an entrepreneur, and live your ideal life.

Your main question at this point may be to know exactly how you will earn income on the Internet. I will be going into a much more detailed discussion of this later on in the book, but for now I want to introduce you to the various business models that my students and I are using in order to bring in revenue with our online businesses. The ones that are used by an overwhelming majority of people working on the Internet today include:

- Information Product Creation
- Affiliate Marketing

- Membership Sites
- Niche Mini-Sites
- Offering Your Services
- Marketing for Local Businesses
- Speaking/Coaching/Mentoring
- Kindle and Amazon
- Combination of these

So, hopefully you can now see that this is a solid and legitimate way to do business, even if you are not familiar with some of these business models. I'll discuss each one in greater detail in a later section.

Online entrepreneurs have become more common since I began in 2006, and with that has come a respect from the more traditional entrepreneurs and small business owners across the globe. People have a difficult time grasping what they are unfamiliar with and cannot see, so once blogs and eBooks and teleseminars became a part of everyday life and went mainstream the stigma of working with electrons as your currency all but disappeared.

Please don't misunderstand me here; this is hard work that requires you to stretch yourself further than you may have ever thought possible. But if you are willing to make a huge effort and persevere, this just might end up being the most exciting and prosperous life you could ever imagine.

Living the Internet Lifestyle

Whether you want to work from a corner of your den or spare bedroom at home or travel the world and work whenever you like from wherever you have an Internet connection, the Internet lifestyle is a worthwhile one.

# What If You Choose The Internet Lifestyle?

If you choose to follow the now tens of thousands of people who have chosen to leave their previous lives behind and come online, you will become a part of a select group of entrepreneurial pioneers. We are people from every walk of life, both men and women, from teenagers to people well into their seventies and beyond, living on six continents, who are seeking a life where we call the shots when it comes to how and when we work, how much we earn, and how and when we interact with others.

My reasons for coming online were based on my desire to change my life for the better and to work with and serve people in need. I did not give a lot of thought to the economy at the time, even though that became a significant factor within a year or so of my getting started as the recession gripped our country and the world. I also did not think about being able to travel, yet that became a huge part of my life within two years of my coming online. I did not ponder the concept of becoming wealthy, yet that is exactly what has happened to me over the last few years. My initial reasons for leaving my previous life, as a classroom teacher and real estate broker and residential appraiser, behind came from a deep seeded need just to survive and thrive each day. It evolved into much more after I made the decision to take a leap of faith and get started.

You have your own reasons for wanting to become an online entrepreneur. It does not matter what they are right now, for they will metamorphose over time as mine have and continue to do. What does matter is your willingness to be open to new ideas, to new ways of expressing yourself, and to new strategies for earning income. If you are open to all of these, your life will begin to unfold in a way you have not previously even dreamed of. I know this because it has happened for me and for hundreds of my students since 2006.

This is a 'recession proof' business model that just makes sense.

Watching my students fall in love with their online businesses continues to be a joyous experience. Many have gone through a job layoff or a serious illness. They go from struggling over which niche to specialize in and agonizing over having to write yet another blog post to becoming almost child-like in their enthusiasm at creating new products and income streams.

# What To Expect

*"You are the average of the five people you
spend the most time with."*
~Jim Rohn

What I did not anticipate was that my everyday life would change so very quickly. I had heard the quote from Jim Rohn I've mentioned above about being the average of the five people you spend the most time with, but it wasn't until I left teaching and real estate in order to pursue my entrepreneurial dreams that I truly understood it. People I was once content to spend time with suddenly seemed like complainers who did not want to improve their circumstances. They continued to blame others – their boss, the government, their former spouse, etc., instead of taking full responsibility for their circumstances.

As I became more positive and willing to change I was less tolerant of those who were stuck in this style of thinking in their lives. And, as I earned more money from my online efforts I realized that I was growing away from the people I had been used to spending time with on a regular basis. When I talked about what I was learning and doing in my new online business, they scoffed at my ideas and made me feel like I could never be successful with this type of business. Soon I simply stopped bringing up the topic, and only spoke about it with a couple of the people who were interested in hearing more about what I was doing and offered their encouragement.

You may have experienced what I am sharing here when you graduated from high school, went away to college, or started a new job. Perhaps we expect our relationships to change in this way with people we knew when we were much younger, but believe it will be different with a more mature group of friends, co-workers, and acquaintances. This was not my experience and I decided that age or life stages did not make any difference at all.

My dilemma was that I did not want my small group of friends to feel like I was abandoning them, yet I was unwilling to allow them to drag me down. It turned out that the situation worked itself out naturally, with me getting more involved in my business and with the new people I was meeting online and at live events. Within a year I was hardly spending any time with these former co-workers and friends. Perhaps they have since added me to the list of people they blame for their own shortcomings and disappointments, but I have no way of knowing this for sure and do not give it any thought except when recounting the story as I am doing here.

I met Steadman Graham several years ago, and he said something that stuck with me – 'I don't hang out.' That resonated with me because I was just moving to the place in my life where my time felt very precious and I was no longer willing to wile it away on activities and with people who did not take responsibility for themselves and who were constantly focusing on the negative instead of the positive side of things.

In the words of my dear friend and brilliant marketer Barb Ling, "Never gift undeserving people with your greatness."

The big question for me was, 'Now that I'm living this lifestyle, how will I spend my time each day, and where will I share my money?'

That question was soon answered when I got involved, first as a volunteer and then as a member with Rotary, an international service organization that focuses on bringing clean water to people who need it, and with eradicating polio in the three countries where it is still endemic. I thought back to the reason I wanted to change my life in the first place and saw that there was so much need in the world. I knew that groups such as Rotary would provide me with a vision and a structure for what I wanted to be a part of, and that it would be worthwhile for me to work hard in order to play a bigger part in serving.

I can remember a project we did at a place called Carousel Ranch during my first year as a Rotarian. This is a non-profit organization that uses equestrian therapy to help severely disabled children make the most of their lives. As I watched the volunteers work with the children I saw miracles occur before my eyes. Being there when a six year old boy called out for his mother for the first time in his young life, as he sat perched upon a horse brought tears to my eyes. Rotary's motto is "Service Above Self" and that is what I continually strive to do in my own life each day.

This goal also helps me to move forward in my business to do as much as possible to grow it to the next level regularly. Finding that balance between work and play was crucial to my success.

'Do what others won't for the next year;
Be able to live the way others can't, forever.'

This quote, an anonymous one, is one that I will refer to often throughout this book. It exemplifies the way I was able to push through the barriers and limits I had set for myself and on to a more successful way of thinking and living.

Over the years I've seen so many people start and stop their entrepreneurial efforts, only to lose valuable time as they have to start from scratch each time they return to their online business. Working in fits and starts does not give you time to get any traction. By committing to work diligently for the first year, building up your business in a steady and methodical way and laying the proper foundation, you will be able to achieve far more than roughly ninety percent of the people who set about 'making money on the Internet'. It's about far more than this, as you will soon see.

If this lifestyle is still appealing to you, and I sincerely hope that it is, continue reading as I will be explaining in great detail how you can get started on the road to becoming a successful online entrepreneur. In fact, the greater portion of this book takes you step by step through the process of setting up a home-based business where you can work exclusively from your home computer, or from anywhere in the world where you have an Internet connection. My recommendation is that you start a notebook you can keep with you as you read to write down and record your thoughts, ideas, and questions as you work your way through each section of the book.

But first, as with all new endeavors, I want to spend some time on the essentials of why I believe you must quit your job if it no longer serves you, and how doing so will open your eyes to a new world of possibilities and experiences. First, let's talk about how people make us feel and how that can affect everything you do in life.

# How Do You Make People Feel?

*'People will forget what you said.*
*People will forget what you did.*
*But they will never forget how you made them feel.'*
*~Maya Angelou*

This is such a powerful concept. I changed dentists when the one I had been going to insinuated that I was vain about having a yellow tooth showing when I smiled. I stopped doing business with a JV partner after he made me feel like I made too much money to care about being paid on time. I started going to a new gym when the previous one made me feel like I was making excuses for not lifting more and more weights each week.

I can't remember exactly what any of these people said or did to make me feel that way, but I do remember exactly how it made me feel at the time. It was a feeling of not being heard, and of being made to feel *less than* others. It was powerful enough to make me take my business elsewhere, and that is enough reason to want to understand how we can make people feel cherished and valued when we connect with them as online entrepreneurs.

Because we almost never do business in person, we must be highly sensitive to the communications we are sharing and the interactions we have with the people who have placed their trust in us to be their trusted advisor.

When someone emails me, messages me on Skype or Facebook, or sends me a letter, I spend time reading and understanding the message before I respond. This helps me greatly with communication, and also serves to help eliminate the possibility of misunderstanding and miscommunication. A quick response is likely to change the tone of what the original message was about and lead to someone feeling bad in the process.

I find that the very best way to communicate is to speak with the other person. This can be accomplished so easily now that there really is no reason not to do this regularly. Speaking on the phone or through Skype gives us the opportunity to listen and truly hear each other. Think about this as you embark on your own entrepreneurial journey.

# Quitting Your Job – Stress Kills

You may have heard many times that stress is a silent killer. Even if you don't believe you are stressed out, or feel the physical and psychological effects of stress, it is there in the background of your daily life, making everything you do potentially life changing in a negative way.

I am certainly not an expert in this area, but I have lived long enough to see the indications and effects of being so stressed out that you are unable to function in a productive way for months or years on end. It happened to me while I was teaching at one school right after the horrific 9-11 crisis in 2001. I have no way of knowing if that event, and the events that occurred immediately afterwards, had any direct connection or correlation with what I went through, but the teachers and administrators at that school became people I did not want to spend time with because of their words and actions. Unfortunately, when you are an employee there is not much you can do, especially when your family is depending on you to bring home a paycheck to cover your day to day living expenses.

Over the next two years I experienced situations that I could never have predicted would occur in a school setting.

I will spare you the sad and gory details, but suffice it to say that people can behave very badly when they are under stress. I found myself saying and doing things that were completely out of character for me as a way of coping with people and situations around me. It was as though I had to be on guard every moment to deflect any possible verbal attacks from some of the adults working at the school. The only strength I found during this time involved shielding the children from direct verbal and psychological abuse each day.

Things got much worse before they got better, and it was during this time that I realized I had put myself in a potentially dangerous situation that I could not easily walk away from. In 2002 I suffered a serious injury at school when I took a fall. I had been standing on the sink in the back of the room in order to hang a bulletin board. I lost my balance and down I went. Within a few months I had rotator cuff surgery on my shoulder and knee surgery to repair a torn meniscus.

For several months I was out of work and collecting Worker's Compensation. That was one of the lowest times in my life, and I knew that being under this type of stress for an extended period of time was dangerous to my overall health and well-being. It would be six full months before I was back to work on a full time basis and catching up with the income I had lost. Just thinking about that period in my life reminds me of how stress set me back in my pursuit of the life I wanted to enjoy.

It is my firm belief that working at the wrong job for you is the culprit for the majority of the stress in our lives, and that by changing our work habits and environment we can eliminate this stress to the point of becoming happier and healthier for the remainder of our life.

Think back to when you were first working at a job. For me, that was when I first worked in restaurants. Making money was lots of fun, but it wasn't necessary in order to keep a roof over my head and food on the table. Imagine being able to go back in time to a more care-free lifestyle when it comes to work.

This was during my teenage years, back in the 1970s, when I worked as a waitress in order to earn spending money. Back then it was common for young people to quit jobs frequently without giving it much thought or discussing the situation with anyone. I had friends at that time who had quit their job, taken another one, and later on returned to the original company they had left previously, all without ever being questioned or judged as to their motives for doing such a thing.

One summer I worked at three different restaurants and no one ever questioned my reasons for leaving one job and moving on to the next. If I was not happy where I was working, for one reason or another, I simply found another restaurant that I considered to be superior to where I was currently working. Most of the time this had to do with the hours I had been assigned to work, the management, the amount of money I could earn in tips, and the proximity to the bus line.

During this particular summer I started out working the graveyard shift at a place called Ranch House, left and took a job working afternoons and evenings at the International House of Pancakes (IHOP), and finally switch to a different IHOP a few miles away.

I'm not sure what state the economy was in back then because I was brand new to the work force and had nothing to compare it to. It was the late 1960s, during the Viet Nam war, and inflation was high. Every time you went to the grocery store it seemed like prices were higher than the time before. Like I said, this seemed perfectly normal to me because I was young and new to being an active member of a household. The answer seemed to be to continue to earn more money so that the rising prices would not become an issue.

As we get older, life takes its twists and turns and many times we end up at a job or in a career that never really suited us. I never thought that would happen to me, but it did. After graduating from UCLA in 1977, I decided to take a year off before going on to graduate school. I was married at that time, and helping to raise my two young step-children, Matthew and Amanda.

Originally I had dreamed of becoming a veterinarian. I loved animals so much and wanted a career where I could devote my life to helping them. But it was not to be. I worked at a veterinary office for a year when I first started college. The pain and suffering the animals endured was simply too much for me to see on a daily basis. After almost passing out while observing a leg amputation being performed on a collie, and having to hold down a rabid dog while he was euthanized all took its toll on me. I changed my major and decided that I would be better off doing something else and just having lots of pets of my own to care for.

I also dreamed of becoming a professional writer at that time, but a few rejections and setbacks was all it took for me to give up on that dream as well.

Unfortunately, I did not have a role model or mentor to help me with my major life decisions and choices, and I was simply not strong enough to do it on my own. I was living my life by the trial and error method, and that does not work very well most of the time.

The real point I am making here is that you are more than likely stressed to one degree or another by the work you are doing, and you are the only one who can change that situation to improve the quality of your life if that stress is more than you can bear.

I appreciate the struggles I've gone through in my life, primarily because if things had not been quite as bad at the time I might still be in those same situations. Instead, I was encouraged to put in the time and energy necessary to get me to the thoughts and actions I have taken to change my life up to this point.

These struggles include being a cancer survivor multiple times, losing my home and nearly all of my belongings in Hurricane Andrew in south Florida in 1992, and losing several people in my family who passed away much too soon.

My first year working online – 2006 – was also a struggle for me. The learning curve was steep and I had cashed out my retirement account through the California state teachers retirement system (STRS) in order to have money to pay my bills that year. The pressure was on because once that money was gone there was no place for me to turn for financial assistance.

My biggest fear was that I would lose my home and not have anywhere to live with all of my animals. I allowed that fear to consume me until I took hold of it and faced it head on. That was when I began taking massive action and treating my new endeavors as a business instead of as a hobby. I also sought out intelligent, kind people to help guide me in the direction I wanted to head in to build the business I was dreaming of.

What about you? Is the stress in your life too much for you to deal with? Are you struggling with finances or relationships or health issues at this time in your life? If so, do not be afraid to ask others for guidance. You'll find that people are actually thrilled to help you move past your crisis and on to success.

# My Typical Day

My time was never my own while I was working for others, or even during the time I had my own small business as a real estate broker and residential appraiser. I had to dance to the tune of the time schedules already established, with almost zero flexibility. Perhaps that is why I value my time so much these days and treasure the moments when I am doing exactly what is important to me.

These days I go back and forth between two homes, and I also travel about one week each month either to speak at or to attend a live event of some kind, typically a conference, seminar, or workshop geared at teaching people how to become online entrepreneurs. In addition, I host private retreats every other month and put on my own live workshops twice a year.

A typical day begins early for me when I am at my home in Santa Clarita, California, a desert community about forty miles north of Los Angeles. I have five little dogs and a cat, and they like to get up by about six each morning. The funny thing I've learned about animals is that they like to get up very early, but after they've gone outside and had a drink of water they like to go right back to sleep. I leave them downstairs and also go back to sleep until around seven or so.

The time when I am the most wide awake and alert is from around seven in the morning until ten-thirty or eleven. I refer to this as my 'prime time' hours and encourage you to find out when your most productive time of the day is each day as well. In this way, you will be able to manage your time more easily and be far more productive on a regular basis, enjoying your life as an entrepreneur even more. I have discovered that being disciplined and adhering to a strict schedule is crucial to maximum success.

So it's off to the computer for me for the next couple of hours most mornings. I start by writing an email to send out to my list, and then I work on blog posts, my next book, and products I am reviewing or creating. You'll notice that I do not check my email, go into forums, or visit social media sites until after I have done some work to move my own business forward; this is an important part of the process of being in charge of and responsible for your own destiny and future.

Around ten or so I usually leave for the day, because working online is just one part of my life these days. I enjoy volunteering for several charities and other non-profit organizations, as well as spending time with friends and family members. I've been a Rotarian since 2006, and

Rotary is an international service organization that has brought new meaning to my life. There are also other groups and organizations I belong to and volunteer with, including the Elk's, a national group devoted to helping the local community and disabled children and veterans, and Zonta, an international women's business organization whose mission it is to advance the status of girls and women around the world.

Once or twice a week I host a webinar for my students during the afternoon on a weekday. I don't have quite as much energy during this time of the day, so sometimes I take a nap right before the webinar is set to begin.

In Santa Barbara I go for a walk when I arise, which is usually around seven or eight. It's very quiet at my house there because there are usually no dogs or other people with me while I'm there. I live near the Santa Barbara Mission, and love walking through the rose gardens and around the magnificent surroundings to start my day. Then I go home and write for an hour or so before heading down to the beach to sit down with a book (I prefer paperbacks, but sometimes bring my iPad Mini) and listen to the ocean waves crashing gently to the shore. Later in the day I go to one of our Farmer's Markets to pick up some healthy foods. Some days I volunteer at the Food bank or at the library. Even though Santa Barbara is a very small town, there is much work that needs to be done when it comes to serving others in need.

# It Wasn't Always This Way

But it wasn't always this way. During my first year and a half I was busy building my business from the ground up, so I was much more likely to sit in front of my computer for eight to ten hours each day during that period of time. I was so new to the idea of being an online entrepreneur that I believed it was necessary to spend every waking moment at my desk. This is what I think of as working 'in' your business rather than working 'on' your business.

If I wasn't watching a training video or listening to an audio recording, then I was writing another article or a post for one of my ten blogs. It was exhausting, but I kept telling myself that at least I was not having to commute many miles each day back and forth to school leave my house at the crack of dawn, fight the traffic into the city to get to school, and then drive to my real estate appointments after school was over each day. Also, I could take a break whenever I wanted or needed to have one.

These times were also the 'dark ages' in terms of having an online business, with no social media and no local groups to connect with. Once Facebook went mainstream around 2007 and Twitter became active by the end of that year, it was much easier to have people to ask your questions to and to share your ideas with virtually around the clock. It's always first thing in the morning somewhere in the world!

When I think back to these early days I have no regrets; for me, learning the discipline of staying focused on building my business was just what I needed at that time in my life. I think of that period as one in which I laid the foundation of my online empire. Engaging in this type of focused discipline each day turned me into a writer, something I had always wanted in my life, as well as someone who thinks ahead and plans three steps into the future. I was quite productive as I learned what worked and what did not, and my time management skills also increased exponentially.

It wasn't until 2008 that I made the conscious decision to only work for about three or four hours each day. This came about after I attended my first Internet marketing event, Armand Morin's Big Seminar, in April of that year. I had not previously attended any events because of the cost involved, but once I went to Atlanta for Big Seminar I realized that it would be worth every penny to attend live events on a regular basis. The training I received, the people I connected with, and the time away from my computer were just what I needed in order to move on to the next level in my business.

As soon as I got home from Big Seminar I changed the way I worked. No longer would I be tethered to my computer for hours on end. Instead, I began working in blocks of ninety minutes at a time, with breaks in between. This was based on some time management and productivity skills that I was just beginning to implement on a daily basis. Four of these ninety minute segments produced as much as working twice as long had produced before. I was organized and focused and that made all the difference in the world.

These practices have been so effective for me that I co-authored a book on the topic in 2011, entitled *Time Management Strategies for Entrepreneurs: How to Manage Your Time to Increase Your Bottom Line*. In it, Geoff Hoff and I go into great detail about how you can achieve more in less time and use these techniques to build a business that suits your lifestyle.

So, why did I end up working on the Internet? When I was searching for an answer to what I could possibly do to earn an acceptable living from home I researched everything I could find. First, I thought back to my own experiences and to those of people I knew. When real estate was slow and I needed to replace my weekend income I had done a couple of things from home that brought in some money.

A friend and I had sold toys on eBay during 1999 and 2000 and I knew that this did not appeal to me. Both of us had garages filled with boxes and shipping materials, we were always trying to find products at a price that would allow us to earn some profit, and the process of sending out physical products all over the world had so many customer service issues. Once we sold our last inventory in December of 2000 we both agreed to call it quits.

I had also sold computers and accessories at the swap meets throughout southern California for about six months during 2001. Almost every Saturday some friends and I would get up at three in the morning to pack the truck and make the trip to one of the swap meets. Then we would set up our tables and set out our merchandise to be ready for the people who would attend the event over the weekend.

This meant that we had to stay in a nearby hotel and get up early again on Sunday to return to our booth. There were so many nice people who were looking for low priced computers, printers, and other accessories, but our margins were low and many times I only cleared about a hundred dollars for the weekend after all of the expenses were paid.

Soon after we began this part-time business the 'big box' companies started selling brand name computers at prices much lower than ours, so we quickly sold the remainder of our inventory and stopped doing this for good. There was also the threat of a lawsuit from a large vendor who claimed we were selling proprietary computer parts, but fortunately they backed down when they saw that we had not done what they were alleging.

You would think after all of these experiences that I would have learned my lesson about trying to become a successful entrepreneur, but once you allow yourself to entertain thoughts of working for yourself in this way it's next to impossible to give them up. I was determined to find some type of business that would work for me so that I could have a better and easier life.

In 2002 I suffered a work injury I mentioned earlier that really made me take a step back and evaluate my life. I was working in my classroom at school and fell while putting up a bulletin board in the back of my room. I had climbed on the sink to be able to reach the place I wanted to place it more easily, and lost my footing when I went a little too high up. The result was a rotator cuff injury to my shoulder and a torn meniscus to my knee.

Over the next six months or so I had surgeries for both of these injuries, endless hours of physical therapy, and was unable to work at both my teaching job and my real estate business for most of that time. I had never been through the Worker's Compensation system, and soon saw why it is such a political issue in many states, particularly in California. I won't bore you with the details here, but suffice it to say that collecting a check each month while you are injured is an experience I do not wish on anyone.

During this time I realized that I had to find something to do that did not require physical strength, driving long distances, or dealing with shipping packages. I would lie on my bed and pray for God to help me find some type of work I could do from home, from my bedroom, if necessary, that would earn me as much money as I needed to meet all of my financial obligations with grace and ease. I prayed this prayer every day, sometimes many times throughout the course of a day, and knew that my prayer would be answered when the time was right.

The answer to my prayer would come three years later, in 2002 and it involved the Internet in a big way.

I had attended a seminar where they gave everyone who attended a large package of CDs to take home. These were the recordings of previous presenters at the seminar, on a variety of topics. Almost immediately I began to listen to these in my car while I was driving back and forth to work and to my real estate appointments. Turning my car into a 'rolling classroom' seemed like a good idea even back then.

One day in November of 2005 I heard one that resonated with me in a big way. It was a man who spoke about being able to set up websites to sell information on topics such as giving a speech at a wedding or for a eulogy, learning how to break into specific careers, applying for a U.S. passport, or how to use PowerPoint to give a presentation at work or for an organization.

He was spending time doing the research on these topics and then outsourcing the actual writing to freelance writers for a few hundred dollars. The CD was only about forty-five minutes long, but it got the wheels of my mind turning in an entirely new direction.

Within a few weeks I had signed up on the lists of several people who were involved in teaching Internet marketing, and I jumped in to get started as quickly as I possibly could. However, I had not anticipated that the learning curve would be so steep or that the technology required would be so difficult for me. I'll share more on that, later on in the book.

# Every Day Is Thursday

I like to say that every day is a Thursday for me now. I used to say every day was Saturday, but Saturdays can be very busy with running errands and catching up with things that didn't get done during the week. The streets and the stores are packed with people who work Monday through Friday and must make the most out of the weekends to be ready for the work week again on Monday morning. Thursdays are more quiet and peaceful in comparison, and that's more like what a typical day is like for me these past few years.

I am reminded here of a scene from the public television series Downton Abbey. Cousin Matthew comes to live at the Crawley Estate in the English countryside, and the master of the house, Robert Crawley is concerned because Matthew has taken a job and will not be available during the week to help run the estate.

Matthew tells Robert and his mother, Lady Grantham (portrayed to perfection by the inimitable Maggie Smith) not to worry about this because he will have plenty of time on the weekend to be involved with the running of the estate. They are speechless until Lady Grantham finally leans in to ask 'What is a week-end?' This just goes to show how people think of things from a variety of perspectives. If every day is Thursday, then you don't think of Saturday and Sunday in the same way any longer.

As an employee for the school district I almost never had the time to do the things I wanted to do. Other teachers spoke frequently about everything they wanted to do once they retired, but I was not willing to work for forty years in order to live the life I dreamed of living. I wanted the best of both worlds; to be involved with work I loved while also serving others and living my ideal life. After surviving cancer more than once and recovering from my serious work injury, I understood that life can go by very quickly and that our time is our most valuable asset and resource.

Being able to shift my time so that I can do everything I want to do is a tremendously valuable gift. For example, on a recent weekend I was co-chairing the Women in Service awards luncheon, so I did absolutely no work at all in my business on Friday and Saturday. Instead, I worked for about four hours on Sunday afternoon to accomplish the goals and tasks I had set for myself for the week. I also have several people who help me on a part-time basis. They are referred to as Virtual Assistants, or Vas for short. You will have this kind of help as well as your business grows larger.

Imagine having the time to attend every school and sports event for your children or grandchildren; joining a charitable organization to help others in need, both financially and with your time; being able to meet a friend for lunch whenever you feel like it; and having the time to grocery shop or hit the sales at your favorite store when everyone else is at work so you have the place to yourself. That's what time shifting allows you to do, and this will be a part of your daily life as an online entrepreneur.

# Travelling the World

I had always wanted to travel the world, but had pushed that thought to the back of my mind for most of my adult life. Except for a few trips within the United States and two trips to Europe in my early 40s, I did not have the time or the money to travel to any of the places I had dreamed of being able to visit. I was surrounded by people who spoke of winning the lottery as the answer to their financial problems, but I was more interested in finding a way to make my own luck and to have more control over my financial future.

The Internet lifestyle has allowed me to pick up and go any time I like. I've ridden elephants in Thailand, cruised the islands of the Caribbean on multiple occasions, helped a friend mark something off his 'bucket list' by arranging a trip to see the Bird's Nest in Beijing, China, and spent the weekend in London seeing the sights. Planning trips where I can combine my work, some fun, and helping others is my favorite way to spend my time and see the world.

Having described my typical day, and sharing my thoughts on time-shifting in order to do what you'd like each day, I will also say that you must be disciplined and organized with your time to make this business work for you. This type of structured life is one that will allow you the freedom to pursue your goals and dreams in a way that leaves you feeling refreshed, fulfilled, and reinvigorated on a regular basis. Allow me to explain what I mean by this.

I never thought of myself as someone with any type of attention deficit disorder. For twenty years I taught children, many of whom presented with various traits associated with attention deficit, but the thought never even crossed my mind that I might have been dealing with this same issue in myself as well. Instead, I went through each day doing exactly what was prescribed by the school district.

If I wanted to teach a math lesson first thing in the morning, I pushed that thought away; it was just an accepted fact that math was always taught during the hour right before lunch. If I had a thought about teaching a social studies lesson outside to make it more interesting or relevant to that day's topic, that thought never worked its way to the front of my mind because we always taught academics indoors.

What I'm saying here is that it took me about a year to understand that I had innovative and creative ideas around teaching for all of those years, yet I never acted on them for fear of being chastised by the other teachers and the school administrators. It was my students who taught me that this was a perfectly 'normal' way of thinking and that wanting to do things differently from the way they had always been done was a wonderfully creative idea.

Every few years a new teacher would join our staff and talk about doing things 'outside the box', but they soon learned that this behavior was inappropriate in our system and would not be tolerated within the public school environment. Most of these people disappeared after a year or two and no one ever mentioned them again. The ones who remained in the classroom soon changed their ways, and the old behavior and attitude was transformed into something unrecognizable. Thinking back to those twenty years makes me very sad most of the time.

It was not until I took a one year leave of absence from the school district and worked part-time at a private high school that I realized how different life could be when you led with your thoughts and feelings and acted upon them in a natural way. That's when I became aware of the fact that I indeed had an attention deficit.

I arrived at the high school three days a week at nine in the morning. Having been hired to teach science and technology, it was assumed that we would conduct experiments and research online to better understand this subject matter. But that's not how it worked after the first week.

Instead, the students and I learned in a more natural way. When one boy's father was diagnosed with lung cancer, we spent the remainder of the week learning more about the causes and treatment of this insidious disease. When one girl returned from a family vacation in Aruba we studied the flora and fauna found in that location.

When someone had an idea, whether it was me or one of the students, we went with it, sometimes jumping from subject to subject in a matter of minutes. At the end of each week I would make sure we were meeting the California State Content Standards for the subjects I was teaching, and as long as we were we could continue moving forward.

The point I am making here is that it does not matter whether you start at Point A and move on to Point B, or if you jump from topic to topic throughout the day, as long as you make sure to be productive during your own prime time hours. I am also severely dyslexic and have used that as well to propel me forward in my life by making this work for me. Whether you have difficulty in focusing on your goal or are already accustomed to being more disciplined in your approach to everything you do, you will still be able to move forward successfully as you learn what needs to be done.

As we move through the steps and stages of you becoming an online entrepreneur, know that you create your own destiny and that it is completely up to you to make your dreams come true. There is a multitude of ways to do this; online marketing is simply the one I am recommending as a way to start living your ideal live as quickly as possible.

# Section Two

# Are You One of the 1%?

I stated earlier that entrepreneurship is not for everyone. In fact, it turns out that only about one percent of the population has a personality that is predisposed to this type of working lifestyle. It takes a specific way of thinking to want to become an entrepreneur, and ninety-nine percent of the population just doesn't have what it takes, at least not intuitively.

What about the rest of us? I state it in this way because I am not one of the one percent. Yes, I started businesses as a young teenager, but that could be considered situational; my mother and I needed more money for the basic necessities of life and I found a way to bring in some quick cash so we could buy what we needed in order to survive.

Later on I naturally gravitated towards the security of a job and believed that this way the way to fit into society and lead a good life, whatever that meant. Even when I started working in real estate I preferred to work for someone else in their office rather than start my own company. Perhaps I craved the security, or at least the *perceived* sense of security of having a job with a company that would handle many of the issues I did not want to learn about and face on my own. Again, it was only out of financial necessity that I finally started my own real estate company and became totally responsible for my business.

Making the decision to leave the world I was familiar with and move completely out of my comfort zone was not an easy one. I wanted to change my life and my destiny and saw this as the path that would take me there. Within a year I realized that I could be successful with this if I learned as much as possible, connected with others already doing what I wanted to do, and persevered in my efforts every single day.

This was the very first time in my life where I made the decision to do something and stayed with it long enough to see it through to success. If only I had been willing to do that during the first fifty years of my life, things could have been much different for me. But I have absolutely no regrets at all. I understand now that everything comes to us over time and that having patience is truly a virtue to be admired and refined.

By now you can see that it's possible to make that transition from being an employee and/or a small business owner to becoming an entrepreneur. Most of what is required is a change in your mindset, which is the way we think about, perceive, and interpret the world around us. Once you understand this sufficiently you can have anything you want out of your life and everything falls into place smoothly and effortlessly; *changing your thinking will change your life*. Please write this down in the journal or notebook you are keeping while reading this book; the statement I just made is a keeper!

# Being Alone With Your Thoughts

I truly believe that in order to be successful as an entrepreneur, or in any area of your life, you must first learn how to be alone with your thoughts. What I mean by this is that you need to be able to sit by yourself and originate the thoughts and ideas that are yours alone; not influenced by any outside sources, such as other people, the media, and situations that are beyond your control that cause fear to overtake you and crush your goals and dreams.

Giving yourself the ultimate gift of listening to your inner thoughts and intuition will allow you to know yourself better than you ever have in the past. Getting to know yourself from the inside out is the first step to getting to like and honor yourself, and then anything is possible in your life.

During my younger years I did not like to be alone. I was an only child and felt like I grew up being alone much of the time, so as a teenager and young adult I sought out the company of others on a regular basis. This led to my spending time with people with whom I had little or nothing in common, having the television or radio on as 'background noise', and spending endless hours walking through crowded shopping malls just to feel like I was not so alone in the world.

Fortunately, those days are in my past, and now I love to be alone in my home, in nature, and even sometimes when I go to a movie, restaurant, or a theatrical performance. I cherish the hours I have to myself each day to write, read, study, and think, as well as to observe how a variety of different situations affect me. Being alone to think and work also helps me to appreciate even more the time I do spend with the people I care about.

I have heard that you cannot truly love another person until you learn to love yourself. I will add that you cannot truly understand others and how the world works until you understand yourself. I believe this can be best achieved by spending time by yourself.

Learn to love being alone with your thoughts and ideas and you will become much happier and more productive in your personal life and in your business.

# Improving A Little At A Time

*'By the yard, it's hard.*
*Inch by inch, it's a cinch.'*
*~Robert Schuller*

Several years ago I had the opportunity to meet motivational speaker Brian Tracy in person and spend the day with him in a small group setting. I learned many things from him during our time together, including the concept that everything we do as entrepreneurs consists of learnable skills. This was a huge breakthrough in my thinking, and it was at that moment I truly believed that I could learn what I needed to become successful in my business.

He also shared his thoughts about the Law of Accumulation, as well as the Principle of Incremental Improvement.

I learned from Mr. Tracy that if I continually learned, upgraded my skills, and set priorities on my daily business activities I would increase my overall productivity and performance by about one tenth of one percent each day, day after day, indefinitely. This formula is called the

1000% formula because if you make these small, incremental changes you could potentially increase your performance and earnings power by up to one thousand percent over the next decade.

If you strive to improve just one tenth of a percent each day, you'll be approximately 26% more productive each year. Instead of thinking about it from a mathematical or statistical point of view, simply focus on learning a little bit each day until you have mastered the skills that currently elude you.

Thinking back to the early 1980s makes me realize that I was an early adopter of computers and technology. This all began when I first heard about word processors around 1982. Having never learned to touch type, it made perfect sense that I would embrace the idea of having a machine that would allow me to make changes to my documents before printing them out. Word processors allowed you to find a word and change it to another word throughout an entire document, and to then save everything on a little disc that was included with the machine. If I had not been willing to spend a little time each day learning what to do, my life today might have turned out quite differently than it has.

Back then my dream was to write stories; short stories, screenplays, theatrical plays, and the like. The problem was that I talked about wanting to be a writer much more than I ever wrote. In fact, sometimes months went on without me writing a word. Then I would sign up for a writing class and pound out something at the last minute to complete the assignments. At some point I decided that my experience mirrored that of writer Dorothy Parker when she said, "*I hate writing; I love having written.*"

Looking back, I certainly wish I had been disciplined enough to write something – anything - on a regular basis, but perhaps I just wasn't in the right place in my life. Instead, years passed without me making much progress in this area, and I seldom finished any writing I started. Even having access to a word processing machine, where I could type and edit and save my documents did not encourage me to get moving towards my writing goals. I can only imagine what may have been if I had understood then Brian Tracy's Principle of Incremental Improvement and had been willing to improve just a tiny bit each day, or at least on somewhat of a regular basis.

When I came online at the end of 2005 I saw very quickly that writing would be a huge part of my business. I would need to write blog posts, articles, short reports, and email messages just to get started. That's when I realized that I could be successful at this online business if I was willing to write, and that writing would become a part of my life at last.

The writing was quite awful at first, but, like everything else we do in life, if you persevere you will improve. I challenged myself to write one hundred articles in one hundred days at the very beginning of my online career, and when it only took me seventy-eight days to achieve my goal I knew that I had turned myself into a writer. This was achieved by getting into the habit of writing each and every day. If I don't write something each day now, even if it's only a blog post, an email to my list, or a handwritten note to a friend or colleague, it feels as though something is missing from my day, as if I had misplaced my keys or forgotten to feed the dogs.

My recommendation is that you embrace the idea of writing as a way to communicate your thoughts and ideas and get your message out to the world. It is quite empowering to know that something you write on your home computer can make an impact on someone halfway around the world within a few minutes of you publishing it to one of your sites.

# Self-Talk

*'Relentless, repetitive self-talk is what changes our self-image.'*

*~Denis Waitley*

Reportedly, we can have as many as seventy thousand thoughts in a single day. If we take away eight hours for sleep, this works out to having a thought approximately every 1.2 seconds. I believe that I am someone with at least a touch of attention deficit, so I may have even more thoughts while I am awake. In this constant and ongoing barrage of stream of thoughts, we are interpreting situations through our filters. There is actually a powerful conversation going on in our minds during all of our waking hours. Psychologists refer to this conversation as 'self-talk' and it can affect everything you do.

According to the studies and books I have read, about seventy percent of this self-talk is mostly negative. If you have low self-esteem, then it is highly likely and probable that your attention is focused far more on the things that you do not appreciate, value, or like about yourself than on your more positive aspects. This little voice inside your head can be a highly critical one until you get it under control.

Upon closer examination of my own daily habits I found that I was engaging in negative self-talk every single morning. During the first ten to fifteen minutes I was awake each day I would say terribly mean things to myself. I would beat myself up in a way that left me feeling worthless, afraid, and unhappy. It was possible for me to become so discouraged by the time I had let my dogs out each morning that I would not pursue any of my goals for the remainder of the day. How was this possible and why did I allow it to continue for so long?

When I started my online business this situation became glaringly obvious because I was now working from home instead of jumping into my car to begin a ninety minute commute. I simply could not afford to feel this way any longer, and because this was all by my hand and of my doing I forced myself to knock it off.

I stood in front of the mirror one morning and stared at my reflection. Instead of allowing any negative self-talk I spoke out loud in a positive manner. I told myself how smart I was and how fortunate I was to now have my own business I could run from home. As a mother would speak to a child, I spoke to myself for several minutes in a way that boosted my confidence and made me feel like I was ready to conquer the world. In effect, I was forcing myself to like who I was and what I was doing, eliminating the negative and accentuating the positive.

I repeated this routine the following morning, and then the next morning, and the one after that. I engaged in positive and uplifting self-talk every single day until it became a part of my morning ritual and was no longer forced or unnatural. It worked.

Spend a few minutes right now, before reading any further to check in with yourself and to say something positive. What can you remind yourself of that you are proud of or excited about? Look into the mirror and smile. Feel the confidence and joy emanating from every part of your being as you engage in positive self-talk for a full three minutes. Don't continue reading until you have done this exercise.

# On Becoming an Entrepreneur

As I explained at the beginning of Section II, not everyone is cut out for the lifestyle of an entrepreneur, but if this lifestyle is one that appeals to you then you absolutely must give it a shot and do whatever it takes to succeed. While I was working in real estate I did not think of myself as being an entrepreneur, and it turns out that I wasn't one at all. Instead, I owned a small business where I was a service provider to those who needed to buy or sell real estate, or to those who needed an appraised evaluation of their property, such as investors, homeowners, banks, mortgage companies, lenders, accountants, attorneys, and the courts. There was no creativity or imagination required on my part as I went about the task of completing my assignments.

It all begins with you starting to *think* like an entrepreneur.

So, what exactly does that entail? Entrepreneurs make things happen, instead of waiting for someone or something else to put the wheels in motion. When I used to describe this to others I would say that when I wake up I'm already at work, but that sounds like a life consumed by work. It isn't that way at all.

Instead, when I wake up I am open to creative thoughts and ideas that will turn into products, courses, and services of my choosing that will be created by me and others on my team. My 'prime time' hours are early in the morning, so it just makes sense for me to get started very quickly after arising each morning at six or seven. By ten or eleven o'clock I am on to other activities that are seldom connected to my work, and once or twice a week I will do some work during the evening hours.

My mind is always turning and imagining what is possible, and everything I do becomes a connection in my brain, synapse to synapse, of what I could create. In other words, if I read the newspaper, have a conversation with someone, or see a movie, my entrepreneur's brain is thinking of how this could become an article, a blog post, a product, or an eBook. It's a subconscious process that makes you many times as productive as you could ever be as an employee, because your business is *your* dream, not someone else's.

As a teacher, my dream was to have my own school one day. But over the years I lost interest in this idea and never took it past the thinking stage. In real estate I was perfectly content to work for others, and only finally opened my own home office out of necessity.

I want to point out here that unless you are willing to make some sacrifices and put some 'skin in the game' you are probably not even close to having the kind of passion and commitment to your ideas that will be necessary. If this is the case, take a step back and give some serious thoughts to the dreams you left behind in previous years. Whatever you can dream and imagine can become a reality. Entrepreneurship can be the vehicle to help you achieve all of your goals and dreams more quickly, using the concepts and methodologies I'm sharing with you in this book.

# So Where Does the Money Come From?

When I hear someone talking about living the Internet lifestyle, I always look to see if I can figure out which business models they are using. Even though the opportunities are vast when you become an online entrepreneur, everything can be traced back to one of the business models we will discuss here in greater detail.

You may be tempted to search for additional methods and techniques, or to pursue 'get rich quick' tactics, but I warn you against that. If it sounds too good to be true, then that is most likely the case. Instead, focus on the strategies used by me and many thousands of others that work extremely well, while also building a business you will be proud to tell others about.

I describe this process as 'getting your plates spinning in the air', where each plate represents another one of the ways you earn money. Start with one strategy, and then expand to others over time. This will always be preferable to starting with several different models at once and not being able to monetize any of them very well because you are not sufficiently focused. I now enjoy eight different streams of online income, but I started out with just one, affiliate marketing.

Here are the different business models I mentioned earlier in this book that are conducive to the Internet marketing lifestyle, and these include:

- Affiliate Marketing
- Information Product Creation
- Membership Sites
- Niche Mini-Sites
- Offering Your Services
- Marketing for Local Businesses
- Speaking/Coaching/Mentoring
- Kindle/Amazon/Create Space
- Combination of these

Let's take a closer look at each one of these, to give you a better idea of which models and strategies fit best into what you may have envisioned as being a part of your own online business.

In my mind, it has always made the most sense to begin with affiliate marketing, and I am not alone when it comes to this way of thinking. When you are just starting out you typically have no products of your own, do not have a clear sense of the process that is involved with an online sale, and need to learn from others who have already been working online for awhile. This was how I started out, and looking back now I see that I had the good fortune to learn from some of the brightest minds working on the Internet during that time, as well as from some people who had many holes in their marketing funnel and were not to be emulated.

Being able to observe how experienced online entrepreneurs ran their businesses, while also earning some money along the way, was the best training ground I ever could have hoped for, and I know my business runs more smoothly today because of this background. I have written a bestselling book on this topic: *Huge Profits With Affiliate Marketing: How to Build an Online Empire by Recommending What You Love.*

Creating information products was the next logical step for me, and that's what I continue to recommend to my students. It gives you credibility in your niche that will never be possible if you are only recommending other people's products as an affiliate. I'll talk more about this a little further in the book.

Membership sites came next for me. When I created a product on how to get targeted traffic to your sites I decided to set it up in a membership site. The product was delivered in this way, and over time I added more content to bring in new members. This is definitely the fastest way to creating passive and residual online income.

Niched mini-sites are a way to earn money with your hobbies and interests, and to also start including your friends and family members. One of my friends is a model train enthusiast and now has sites in this niche. My grandkids love skateboarding and I helped them to start their own sites devoted to this topic. Now they earn their own spending money and one of them is quite interested in becoming an entrepreneur in his own right as he reaches adulthood.

Offering your services makes sense if you need to start earning income from the very beginning. Make a list of your skills and experience and then offer this to people who need your help. This is exchanging time for money, but it's an excellent way to fund your training as you build your own online business. Over time you can begin to outsource the actual work involved in the service to others, freeing up your time and helping other people to achieve their own dreams and goals by earning income on the Internet.

Local business marketing is an area I fell into accidentally. I had a family member who had started a handyman service and was spending hundreds of dollars each month on advertising. I offered to set up a simple Wordpress site for him and to write some articles and soon he was getting all of his business from the Internet. He stopped advertising in the local newspaper and magazines within a couple of months and has never looked back. Soon after I began marketing for him an insurance agent came to me to help him with his business, and it wasn't long before

I had several small business clients. Your goal is to make their phones ring, and they take over after that.

Coaching or mentoring gives you the opportunity to give back to others in a way you may find very rewarding. My background as a classroom teacher made this a perfect way for me to continue helping others to learn. This will take a time commitment that you must be willing to stick to if you decide to do this. Another way to coach or mentor is to offer classes with a fixed start and end date, allowing you to work closely with people only for a specified period of time you wish to make yourself available to them.

Amazon became one of my income streams in 2010 with the publication of my first book. Before that time I had made a few affiliate sales with them, but now I see it as a huge source of revenue. With my own eight books, other people's books, and many physical products to recommend on Amazon, it makes sense to add this as an income stream as early as possible.

# The 5 Pronged Approach™

Now let's get down to the nuts and bolts of creating your online business. In 2008 I came up with my original 5 Pronged Approach™ for building a profitable online business. Many things changed over time, so in 2013 I updated this to an all new version of this powerful concept and strategy. I'll explain it in more detail here for you. Each prong is intended to help you gain visibility and credibility in your area of specialization.

1. Blogging/Self-Publishing Books - Your blog is your 'Home on the Internet'. This is where you share more about who you are, what you do, and how you serve others in your business. You will set up your blog using hosted Wordpress, so you will own your site and have complete control over what you publish there. Blogging may seem tedious at first, but trust me when I say that it is the single most powerful way for you to reach others who are interested in you and in your topic.

   Writing and publishing books is the natural and logical evolution for the content you are creating within your blog posts, and that has never been easier to do. With the advent of Amazon's Kindle and Create Space programs for self-publishing, you now have a way to get your ideas, information, and expertise out to the world. I have quite a few books available in both paperback and on Kindle and will continue to use this strategy to build my business. This also puts you in the favorable position of being a content publisher.

2. Short Reports - Previously I taught that article marketing was the second prong in my approach, but that all began to change at the beginning of 2011 when Google changed its algorithms. Although I will continue to write and submit a few articles to the directories each month, my primary focus has been to repurpose my content over to short reports instead. These reports can be sold or given away, and will continue to bring you credibility, visibility, and income for years to come when you include links to your own or to some relevant and appropriate affiliate products.

3. Teleseminars/Audio/Podcasts - Allowing people to hear your voice is the next best thing

to meeting them in person. Use a variety of modalities to make sure you are heard discussing your niche topic on a regular basis. I continue to host teleseminars each month, and also have two regular podcast series available as a free subscription in iTunes. Interviewing others and being interviewed by those in similar or complimentary niches will also extend your reach exponentially over time.

4. Social Media/Forums/Live Events - I started my online business during the 'Dark Ages of Social Media', which means that there was no social media to speak of during 2006 and into 2007. I did spend time on a few forums at that time, and found out quickly which ones were worthwhile. I now recommend that you spend no more than twenty minutes each day on the 'Big Three' social media sites – Facebook, Twitter, and LinkedIn – and that you join one or two paid forums to connect with others. Also, be sure to set up your channel over at YouTube. Attend live events whenever possible, starting with those in the city where you currently live and branching out to the bigger ones around the country later on. If you are on another continent than North America, Google for the

events that will be coming to a city hear you. Our business is global, so there is always a live event being put together somewhere in the world. Meeting people in person is the ultimate way to socialize for your business.

5. Affiliate Marketing – This makes the most sense for you if you are a new online entrepreneur and have no products of your own, or only a few, at this time. I am now what is referred to as a 'Super Affiliate', which means that I can win many affiliate contests, drive significant traffic and sales to promotions I believe in, and earn a mid five figures a month, every single month, just from my affiliate promotions. This all started in the spring of 2006, when I made my first affiliate sale of a niche eBook and earned twenty-one dollars and sixty cents. I saw the possibilities immediately and took off with this business model. People come to me regularly to help them launch their products and programs, and I teach affiliate marketing to those who want to learn how to do this in their own online business.

This is the 5 Pronged Approach™ I first created back in 2008 and I stand by this updated version. Go through each step carefully and see what you need to add to your current marketing plan. Do not leave out even one of these prongs or your business efforts will not be nearly as effective.

# What's For Sale?

Right now I would guesstimate that there are *at least* ten thousand ways for people to purchase something from me on the Internet. What I mean by this is that I have almost two thousand articles circulating on thousands of sites, more than fifteen hundred blog posts on my two main sites, more than a hundred short reports, several hundred autoresponder messages, and more than three hundred of my affiliates who are actively promoting one or more of my products with an affiliate link. My educated guess may actually be quite conservative when you think about how so much of what we say and do online goes viral within our niche.

This means that I have much more of an opportunity each day to actually earn money without making any additional efforts because there is already so much for sale out in cyberspace that is either one of my own products or services, or something created by someone else that is attached to my affiliate link.

A couple of years ago I was speaking at a conference in Atlanta – the NAMS (Novice to Advanced Marketing Strategy) event - and the day before it began I met with a group of my students who were attending this event for the first time. We had a roundtable discussion and I asked them what their biggest frustration was when it came to building an online business. They all agreed that it was the difficulty they were experiencing in trying to make money exclusively from their efforts on the Internet.

When I asked each of them this question – "What's for sale?" – it turned out that many of them had next to nothing at all available for sale either as their own product or service, or even through an affiliate link!

That's when I realized that new entrepreneurs were not seeing the direct correlation between making money online and having something available for sale on the Internet. Many of them seem somewhat amazed when I explained that money has to change hands before anyone gets paid, and that you must be selling something or promoting an affiliate product before you can earn money online. My group at this even quickly got my point and we spent the next couple of hours discussing how they could do this in a way that would serve others in their niche.

Ask yourself this question every single day, and continue to get your name, your information, and your links out to the world. Start with your blog, and use this as a springboard to letting the world know who you are and what you have to offer them. The more high-quality products and services you make available, the more income you will earn.

We will explore this concept more thoroughly in the next section. Make sure you are keeping a written journal of your thoughts, ideas, and questions as you read through this book.

# Section Three

# Getting Started

*'Don't wait; the time will never be just right.'*
*Napoleon Hill*

Being able to work from your home computer, or from wherever in the world you happen to be is truly a gift from God, in my opinion. Back in the early 2000s, when I was home in bed after having my cancer recur for the second time, as well as recovering from a serious work injury, I asked for divine guidance in my life.

My prayer each day was to find a way to work from home, from my bedroom if necessary, and to be able to earn enough money to meet all of my financial obligations with grace and ease. Little did I know the answer would come several years later, while I was listening to some CDs in my car as I drove back and forth to school and to my real estate appointments.

I had purchased a package of training CDs after attending an event in Los Angeles in 2005. There were more than fifty of them, so each Monday morning I would load six of them into my car's CD player so I could listen to the trainings during that week. Some of them were interviews with entrepreneurs and thought leaders, others were on topics I had no interest in (but I listened to them all the way through anyway to get some nuggets I would have otherwise missed entirely), and some were recordings of presentations that had been given at the same event I attended, but in years past.

One of these in particular got my attention. It was the recording of a presentation on how to set up two page 'mini-sites' to sell information on a variety of topics. Some of the examples they used were public speaking, dog training, wedding speeches, and eulogies. As I listened I became more and more excited about the possibilities of creating this type of business that could be run entirely from my home computer.

Within days I had started thinking about this in a way that I had never done before. It was as though I had won the lottery, but more exciting because I would be creating something based on my own ideas and efforts that would have nothing at all to do with luck. I was ready to change my life and make my own luck from now on.

With my limited budget at the time, I searched on eBay to see what I could find on this topic. To my delight there were many books and CDs available on how to get started online, and though my bids were low I won many of the auctions for these materials. I spent about a hundred dollars in all and the packages began arriving at my door. This was in November of 2005, and my education and new adventure was about to begin.

Little did I know at that time that this would completely change my life, or that the learning curve would be quite so steep. I was game for anything at this point in my life, so nothing else mattered. Can you relate to feeling this way about something in your life at one time or another?

## Residual versus Linear Income

I was interested in building residual income, not simply working each day to create linear income. What I mean by this is that when you have a job you are typically paid a specific amount of money by the hour, by the week, or by the month for the work you do. Except for any paid holidays, vacation time, and sick days your company may provide, if you are not actively working then you are not earning any money. This was my experience as a classroom teacher for twenty years.

The same can be true for many small businesses, such as the one I had set up for my real estate company. Unless I was out physically selling, listing, or appraising a property, I earned no income. From time to time I had other people working for me as independent contractors and doing the actual work, but ultimately it was my responsibility to oversee anything they did before I would sign my name to it.

All of these scenarios describe what is referred to as 'linear' income; money that is earned for work you are actively involved in. It may seem fair that you would only be paid for the work you do, but that's thinking like an employee or small business owner rather than as an entrepreneur. There IS a difference and it is huge.

Residual income is much better! Residual income is money you earn over and over again from work that you have performed only once at some previous point in time. This is a common term in the show business world. When someone is on a television show or in a commercial, they will do the work once and may be paid residuals for years into the future depending upon the deal they negotiated at the beginning.

It works in a similar way in this business; if I write an eBook or a book for Kindle, I need only do that one time in order to make it available for sale for years to come. I still earn money today from books I wrote several years ago. The same concept holds true for information products, courses, niche sites, and membership sites. When I create something new I spend time putting it together once and then earn residual income from it over and over and over again, even from products that I created several years ago.

Your goal must be to do this same thing, in a way that works for you and your online business. I'll explain exactly how you can do this.

## The Three Most Important Things

In order to earn money online, you need three things to get started down the road of online entrepreneurial success. These three things include choosing a niche with a large target audience; building a list of interested prospects and buyers; and setting up a logical profit funnel. Let's talk about each one of these things in greater detail.

You'll want to choose a niche based on what you are interested in, have had some experience with, and where there are many people who are willing and able to purchase products that will help them to solve their problems in this area. Start by making a list or creating a mind map to get your ideas out of your head and down on paper (or on to your computer, if that works better for you).

Here are some of the top niche markets you may want to choose from in the beginning:

- Health and Fitness
- Relationships
- Self-Help and Personal Development
- Hobbies and Collectibles

- Home and Family
- DIY (Do It Yourself)
- Business Training
- Time Management and Productivity

These are very broad in scope, so you will choose a more specific niche within one of these, such as parenting in the broader area of relationships, model trains in the area of hobbies and collectibles, or anti-aging in the broader area of health and fitness. This is also nowhere near being an exhaustive list of niche markets, but simply a starting point for you to understand what is needed for you to begin.

## List Building – 7 Step Process

The next step is to start building a list of people who will be interested in your topic. That is best achieved by setting up a blog to write about your niche and also setting up opt in pages where people can download a free report or other free gift in exchange for giving you their name and email address. Let's call this step one in the process.

1. An optin box on your blog, as I just described above, where you offer a free

report or other giveaway for those who opt in to your list.

2. Stand alone optin pages – These are pages that can be easily set up using the Wordpress platform. The idea here is to attract different segments of your market who may be interested in different things you have to offer.

3. Teleseminar Invite page – This is an excellent strategy to invite people from social media to become a part of your list by offering them a free teleseminar on your topic. The thank you page can direct them to exactly where you call will be held.

4. Live Events – Connect with people at local, national, and international venues and give them a business card or other way to join your list.

5. Forums – Join one or two paid forums and add your blog or optin page URL to your signature line, along with a 'call to action' to make people want to check out what you are doing.

6. JVs – Joint Ventures work very well for list building. Connect with people in similar or complimentary niches and mail for each other's sites so that everyone's list grows.

7. Your product on someone else's thank you or download page – This is a slightly more advanced strategy that I'm now using. Create an inexpensive product or report and ask more established marketers to give it away on their thank you or download page, through their affiliate link. They have the opportunity to earn additional income now and in the future and your list grows.

These are the seven steps I am recommending for you when you are building a list, which needs to be a regular focus for you as you build your online business.

# Your Profit Funnel

The final step is to set up a profit funnel where your prospects can become customers by purchasing what you have to offer them. The only way you will earn money is when someone makes a purchase, either directly from you or through your affiliate link.

If this sounds confusing, sign up on my list or someone else's to see how it all works. In the beginning I found this all to be so confusing I would write down each step of the process and even print out the emails I was receiving from others to get it all straight in my mind. Within a month or so I understood it very well.

So now you may be wondering which types of products people in your target market will purchase from you and what to include in your profit funnel. The secret to finding out what they want is to see what they are already buying.

Don't try to reinvent the wheel or come up with something new and unique. You shouldn't guess at what they want. And do not try to offer people that you think they "need". We all *need* to eat more fruits and vegetables, but we *want* to eat more of the other foods we love.

Here's how to find out what people are already buying in three easy steps:

1. Go to Clickbank.com or JVZoo.com and view the marketplace sections. These are both sites that house thousands of digital products in a wide variety of niches. Either browse the categories or use their search function to search for niche products in your market. Those products at the top of the search results and categories are the bestsellers, but you'll want to look deeper than that to see what else is available. I prefer to recommend something that is helpful and appealing instead of a product that is simply a best seller.

2. Next, go to Amazon.com and run a search for your niche market keywords (like 'anti-aging creams' or 'anti-aging books'). Those products and books appearing at the top of the search results are the most popular products in the niche. Again, be willing to research further to find what else is there. Amazon is the largest marketplace in the world and you may be amazed at what is available there.

3. Finally, enter those same keywords you used on Clickbank, JV Zoo, and Amazon into a Google search and see what shows up in the regular search results as well as the sponsored results. The sponsored results are the paid advertisements at the very top and on the right-hand side of the

results pages. What are the top sites in your niche selling? Write everything down, as this is a crucial part of your research.

Once you complete these three simple steps, you'll know exactly what your market is already buying. First, recommend affiliate products as part of your profit funnel. And then, after you've got a better feel for what you're doing in your business create your own product that either comes before, during, or after the ones other people have created. You can do easily that by studying the competition, finding the flaws in their products, and making sure your product doesn't include those same flaws.

I highly recommend always purchasing a product before recommending it to others. I've even written a bestselling book about this called *Huge Profits with Affiliate Marketing: How to Build an Online Empire by Recommending What You Love.* Owning the product yourself allows you to see the flaws and omissions first hand. You will also want to read the reviews written by others about the product. If people repeatedly mention a weakness of the product, then you'll instantly know how to create a better product.

## A Simple Campaign

Let's use the niche topic of anti-aging as an example of how to set up a simple marketing campaign. We will assume that you have a personal interest in this topic, are already experienced with trying different things to help yourself age more slowly and gracefully, and that there are many products readily available to help people solve both their perceived and real problems with issues related to this topic.

First, start a blog on this niche topic and share as much information as you possibly can with your readers. You are your own best Case Study when it comes to sharing information with others who need help. Add an optin box to the upper right-hand corner of your blog and offer a free report as your 'ethical bribe' to get people to join your list. You will create this free report by writing about your own experiences in some area of anti-aging such as reducing wrinkles, having more energy, or being good to yourself with yoga and meditation. These are just some examples to get you started thinking. Remember that being your own Case Study you will build credibility very easily.

As I just explained in the previous section, search for the keywords for this niche by going to other people's blogs and websites, as well as visiting Google, Amazon, Clickbank, and JVZoo to see which words and phrases are being used to describe and explain this niche.

Use those phrases as your blog post titles, and as titles for the articles and short reports you will be creating over time.

Also, find out who the big names and the 'players' are in this niche. Read their books, listen to their audios, watch their videos, and follow their every move online. People are bound to ask you questions about them, so it's best if you are familiar with what they have to say. Do not be afraid to disagree with their position on key issues in the niche; controversy can be very good for your business. Have a solid reason for feeling the way you do on these topics.

Share your new site with everyone you know, including the people in your personal circle of influence (friends, family members, people in the groups and organizations you are already involved in, etc.), as well as on social media sites such as LinkedIn, Twitter, and Facebook. This will get the ball rolling so that the world will know what you are doing and have to share with them.

Search for the products that you decide would be most helpful to your target audience, remembering that they will most likely purchase things they want, rather than what you might feel they need.

Read the product descriptions and other people's reviews before deciding which three you will purchase for yourself. Base your decisions on which ones appear to be the best product at the best price with the most value for what you are looking for. This is the beginning of putting yourself in your prospect's shoes so that you can have a firm grasp on what motivates them to buy.

Give yourself enough time to evaluate each product properly. For example, it if's a wrinkle cream, you may need to use it for seven or ten days to see what, if any changes occur.

I also want to take a moment to discuss what an evergreen product is right now. Your goal is to promote products, as much as possible, that are evergreen, meaning they will still be available and relevant to your topic a year or two from now. Nothing is forever, but you don't want to be in the position of having to look for new products to promote every month. You will be the best judge of what is evergreen in your market.

Once you decide on a product that is good enough to recommend, write a blog post about it, write an article that you will submit to the article directories, and include it in what will become a short report when you write more in the future. This is called repurposing, which is the process of taking one idea and turning it into as many pieces of content as you possibly can. I like to begin with written content and then repurpose that into audio, video, and more over time. At some point you will have people who will help you with this process. A good virtual assistant can help you to double or even triple your content.

Also, write an email about this product and include it as an autoresponder message that your list will receive on a specific day after opting in to join your list. If you do this once a week you will soon have a residual income stream set up for years to come. I like to choose the broadcast emails that have been most successful for me and add them to the queue for people who join my list at a later date.

You have now successfully set up a simple affiliate campaign, and everything you do to market your business in the future will be based on the principles I've outlined here. Do not leave out any steps or you will make more work for yourself later on. The idea is to be productive and manage your time so that you can enjoy the Internet lifestyle in the way you have been dreaming of since finding out about becoming an online entrepreneur.

Now you want to focus and concentrate on refining your niche, growing your list, choosing more affiliate products, creating your own products, and increasing your own visibility and credibility. We will discuss and explore all of these areas here in this section.

## Refining Your Niche

We'll stay with the example I used above, anti-aging, to go further into the topic of refining your niche. The idea here is to start out broad and general and to go more narrow and specific over time.

Earlier I stated that health and fitness is an excellent niche. This is true for many reasons, and people spend lots of time and money exploring many facets of this topic. You may resonate with this field because of your own knowledge and life experiences and want to go more deeply into an area where you believe you can help the most people. Let's just say that area is anti-aging, and that you feel uniquely qualified because you look very young for your age, get compliments regularly from the people you encounter, and have come up with some of your own tips, tricks, and secrets for staying youthful in both your thinking and your appearance.

You'll want to find as many credible resources as you possibly can on this topic. Visit your public library and read everything they have available. Ask people you know to share their knowledge and experiences on your topic. Subscribe to sites that provide information and resources you will benefit from. On this topic, anti-aging, I receive information from Oprah's site that I might not ever hear about otherwise. Whatever your niche topic, there are already people and resources you will be able to learn from and incorporate into what you have to offer the world. It will be unique because no one else could possibly understand it or explain it from your perspective.

**Opt In Pages**

When I was just starting out with my online business I thought that having an optin box on my blog was enough. It made perfect sense to me that people would find my blog, decide that they wanted to know more, and leave their name and email address in exchange for my free giveaway.

It turns out that your blog's optin box is just the beginning of this process, and that over time you will have many sites devoted to attracting different segments of your audience. For example, staying with the niche topic of anti-aging, you will want to attract both men and women, from around age forty to well into their eighties or beyond, and people with different backgrounds, experiences, and reasons for wanting to get involved in this area for their own benefit. The optin page that would attract someone forty years old who had just discovered a wrinkle or a gray hair would be very different from one that would attract someone who has just celebrated their eightieth birthday and wants to have more energy, stamina, and flexibility.

It has become quite easy to create these web pages using Wordpress, or to have someone more experienced set them up for you. There are a variety of plugins available that will enable you to set up a new optin page in as little as fifteen minutes. Also, once you've done it a few times it will become second nature. As with most everything else in life, taking action and practicing turn work into child's play.

Implementing the strategy of using multiple optin pages to reach different market segments will help you to grow your list more quickly.

## Getting People to Open Your Emails

Growing your list is only the beginning. You need people who will continue to eagerly open your emails, ready for your next tip, story, or offer! Here's what it means to:

Focus on your subscriber:

Before writing a word, ask yourself, "What would educate, entertain, or inspire my reader today?" Choose one of these options and it's as simple as that to get started.

Use Irresistible Subject Lines:

Two components, and two components only, will make your subscriber decide to open your email – even if they are the sort of person that 'doesn't have time' to read.

Number One: Being able to see clearly who the email is from and having a mental picture of how you 'fit in'.

Putting your full name in the 'From' designation is good, but if they've signed up quickly to get a free report on a topic they need, they may not actually remember your name. So make sure you give them another great big clue.

Seeing a 'From' Line that reads 'Connie Ragen Green' may or may not bring up a mental picture of who you are and what you do. Seeing a 'From' line that reads 'Connie Ragen Green | Affiliate Marketing' will certainly jog their memory. However, in the interest of both saving space and branding yourself, you may want to stick to using just your name in the 'From' area.

Number Two: Compelling Subject Lines

*Number One* is easy enough to set up; and once you've done so, you don't need to do this again. It consists of not only making sure your name displays in the 'From' field, but also a clue about what you do.

*Number Two*, creating irresistible and compelling Subject Lines, is a little more work. However, the good part is that you don't have to create the wittiest or cleverest Subject Lines on the planet. Nor do you have to win a Pulitzer Prize for writing.

Your Subject Lines just have to inspire the reader to open them. And here's a secret that everyone should know but too many people ignore - *Every email after your first couple will be opened based not just on the actual promise in the Subject Line – but on whether or not you fulfilled that promise.*

In other words, if your first "Quote of the Day" was pedestrian, your subscriber is less likely to open the next one.

If "News you can't live without!" turned out to be not that spectacular and something your subscriber has already heard from five previous correspondents, your subscriber is most likely to skip the next email.

And if your first free Template turned out to be dependent on purchasing a Toolkit, it's virtually guaranteed your next free offer won't be opened.

Here are a few tips to make sure your Subject Lines do the trick:

Be clear in what the email is about.

For example, 'Here's a review template for you' is much clearer than 'Wanna freebie?'

Make your Subject Line sound conversational rather than like a book chapter Title. 'What my business told me about honesty today' is more likely to intrigue than: 'You and Your Business – What Honesty is Really All About!'

Learn about Spam filters – and the words in your Subject lines that trigger them. Words sure to bounce your emails straight to your intended recipient's spam filter limbo are:

*Free*

*Sale*

*Work at Home*

*Make Money*

*Click install*

*Income*

*Profit*

There are many more, but these will give you the idea; anything that even vaguely hints at sales or sex may be tossed in spam limbo – no matter how pure your intentions are.

Finally, be very careful with punctuation. Avoid exclamation marks and dollar signs like the plague.

Don't use initial caps: Write your subject line the way you would if you were sending a message to your sister or best friend.

Use a Conversational Tone

Not just in your Subject Lines, but in your emails, your blog posts, and your articles, too. Write as if you're speaking only to the person who is reading it and not to the hundreds or thousands of people who may be on your list.

Make your Emails Shareable

Not just information – but *your* information in particular.

And if you want your reader to share your email be sure to tell them that, and then give them a link to send people to, so they can sign up for your list voluntarily.

Track Your Emails

Your email campaigns will never achieve wild success until you use the tools your Autoresponder should provide to track the following data:

*Unsubscribe rates*

*Delivery rates*

*Opens*

*Sales*

Use this data to help you refine and hone each new email you write. For example, your Delivery Rate should provide valuable clues as to which Subject Lines are not getting through Spam filters.

Make a note of possible trigger words in the Subject Lines of emails that weren't delivered and either avoid using them; or use them in a split-test group, to confirm whether or not that certain word is the problem.

## Some Advanced List Building Strategies

I'm well known for making huge profits with a tiny list. I even wrote my first book (*Huge Profits with a Tiny List: How to Use Relationship Marketing to Increase Your Bottom Line*) about exactly how I did this in the beginning and continue to do this in my own business. In fact, I was able to get to six figures a year with a list of only 651 subscribers. I know the exact figure because that's when online marketing strategist and productivity expert Alex Mandossian contacted me to see how I had become one of his top affiliates seemingly overnight for his Teleseminar Secrets training course in the fall of 2007. He was amazed when I told him the size of my list at that time.

However, list building must be top of mind if you are to become a successful online entrepreneur, and we will discuss some excellent ways for you to do this. Every time you send an email people will unsubscribe, so you must constantly be attracting new people and earning their trust.

Long ago, in the years leading up to when I came online, people were so excited about receiving email they would sign up on a list without giving it much thought. Do you remember those days? Well, they have been over for some time now.

In order to get someone to opt in to a permission based list (they are giving you permission to email them for as long as they remain on your list and do not unsubscribe) you must offer them a compelling reason to do so. This is usually in the form of a short report on a specific aspect of your niche. It must be irresistible so they will feel like they absolutely must have this information or the world will come to an end. I'm exaggerating, of course, but only slightly.

Your site must be easily found by your potential prospects for this to all fall into place on a regular basis. Here is what I recommend:

- Blog regularly (about twice a week), using your keywords in your blog post titles and within your posts
- Submit articles to both free and paid directories such as EzineArticles.com, ArticlesBase.com, SelfGrowth.com, GoArticles.com, and SubmitMoreArticles.com, adding your optin page

or blog URL in the resource box at the end of the article

- Connect with people in paid forums and add the URL of your page to your signature line
- Become active on social media sites like Twitter, Facebook, and LinkedIn and share your URL liberally
- Seek out others in your niche to collaborate on JVs (joint ventures) and to share information on your topic
- Interview others and request to be interviewed to extend your reach
- Become an author of books related to your niche topic

Think about list building every day in order to build your list in a steady and methodical way. Even though bigger is better, you will want to attract the right people for your list over time.

## Choosing More Affiliate Products

As time goes on you will want to find even more affiliate products to recommend to your community. The very best products are the ones you have purchased and benefitted from personally, so think about that as you plan what you will market to your community.

I recommend that you only add an affiliate product to your virtual inventory after you have purchased it, benefitted from it, and can feel good about asking others to spend their money on it.

Go back a few pages to the section entitled 'Your Profits Funnel' to refresh your memory on how to find excellent products to recommend to others through your affiliate link.

## Creating Your Own Products

You won't truly be a player as an online entrepreneur until you begin creating your own information products. Start with simple ones that can be created quickly and then move on to more sophisticated ones that you will spend more time and energy putting together.

It took me a full year of working online before I created my first product, simply because the entire process seemed so confusing and complicated in my mind. If you are feeling this way, remember that you have some specific knowledge in your area of specialization that people will be willing to pay you for.

Again, let's take the example of anti-aging. Perhaps people are always surprised and astonished when you reveal your age to them. You may typically answer by saying something like 'it's due to having good genes' or 'clean living is the answer'. No matter what you say, there is a story behind it. You could create a simple product that shares your experience with others so they will have greater insight into how they can do something similar in their life.

This works for any niche you can think of. People are not expecting to have their life transformed overnight, but having more knowledge and a clear idea of what to do next is of great value as they move forward to achieve their goals. Think of your product as one is which people can go from where they are right now to closer to where they would like to be in the near future. It's the 'one problem, one solution' approach to information product creation and is an extremely effective one.

My recommendation is that you create an outline of what you will be sharing in your product, and then create an audio recording and a short report to convey your information to others. You could also create a video, but that is actually my least favorite way to provide or to receive my information. That's why audio and written content are the primary means through which I deliver my information products.

Also, remember that people will only spend money on the things they want, not the ones they need, especially if they do not know you or are not knowledgeable on your topic. To counteract this way of thinking, create a product they want and include in it the exact and specific information you know they need.

Give your product a name that describes it well, such as 'Anti-aging Secrets Through Clean Living', and then purchase that as a domain. You'll use that site to create an optin page with a free giveaway, a short sales letter to describe what you're offering, a thank you page, and a product download page. Over time you'll have many of these sites as part of your online empire. Have fun with this as you share your knowledge with the world!

## Increasing Your Visibility And Credibility

I was able to move ahead quickly in my business because I started early on with trying to find the best ways to get my name out to the world. You have to remember that I started back in 2006, before social media (Facebook was still just for college students, LinkedIn was geared toward the corporate world, and Twitter was just a gleam in the creator's eye) had gone mainstream.

Instead, I did things like introducing myself at the beginning of other people's teleseminars, writing sincere testimonials for other people's books, courses, and products, and joining forums where my potential prospects and clients were spending time. All of these actions enabled me to get in front of the exact people I most wanted to reach, without costing my anything or forcing me to leave home.

This was a good marketing strategy at the time, but these days the competition is much fiercer and things move more quickly. I would encourage you to join paid forums (I recommend the two I belong to that are listed in the Resources section at the end of the book), attend live events, and become active on social media sites to reach a global market in your niche quickly and easily. Again, I will mention that it all begins with your blog, which is your 'Home on the Internet'. We will be discussing credibility and visibility in greater detail in this next section.

# Becoming An Authority

*"It's not enough to be the best at what you do; you must be*
*perceived as the only one who does what you do."*

*Jerry Garcia*

*1942-1995, Musician*

Now that we've covered some basics about getting started as an online entrepreneur to live the Internet lifestyle, let's move on to some advanced strategies. Part of this includes your thinking about the role you play in your business as that of an authority and a publisher.

It would be several years before I understood the power of becoming a content publisher, but I was well on my way to working in a very different way. By making the conscious decision to change my life forever, I had taken the all important first step to becoming an online entrepreneur.

I soon found out that there were so many people attempting to so this same thing on the Internet that I would have to set myself apart from others if I were to be successful in my business. Working hard, learning as much as possible, and implementing what I was learning were simply not enough to stand out from the crowd. The Internet can be a noisy place and you must rise above the din so that people can hear your message. You achieve this by turning yourself into an authority on your niche topic.

The subject of becoming an authority is one I've spoken about at live events around the world since 2010. I'll be sharing that information with you here, as well as giving you more insight into how you can do this quickly by following twelve simple steps. It will take you some time to implement what I'm teaching here, and taking action right away will get you on the path to success.

Here are the twelve steps I recommend:

1. Decide exactly what you want to be known for and don't spend any time at all on being known for anything else. By focusing on this step with intensity you will be able to rise above the crowd almost immediately. With everything you say and do, ask yourself if this is bringing you closer to your goal of being known in your specific niche or further away from it.

2. Be seen in the right places, both online and in person. This would include attending workshops, seminars, and other live events, as well as publishing on your blog, in magazines and other publications, on social media sites, in videos, and with podcasts and teleseminars. Remember to

consider where your prospects would be searching for people to learn from, ideas to implement, and for information on their topic of interest, rather than simply your colleagues and clients.

3. Show others your credibility quickly. You most likely already have training, certifications, degrees, previous work experience and more, so share that with your prospects. Ask people who know you to give you endorsements and testimonials as to the kind of person you are and what you have done to enrich their lives. Use storytelling to share your life history with others and show yourself as knowledgeable and credible.

4. Publish content on your topic. This includes articles, blog posts, online and offline publications, and more. Create a strategy for this to show others you are an authority one piece of writing at a time.

5. Create, or have created for you, a consistent look and feel to everything you are doing. People make their decision about who you are within nanoseconds, so make sure that first impression is a memorable one. Blink by Malcolm Gladwell, craft the context in which you are seen, website, business cards, logo, develop a consistent look and feel, layout

6. Become a visible marketer. Engage in a guerilla campaign, blog, "newsmaster" (write about other

people's posts and link to them), do this 4-5 times a week (3-4 times about someone else's post and the rest are your own posts), engage in strategic linking, use social media here as well

7. Leverage the power of the Internet with repurposing. – blog post to podcast to article to tweets (RSS) to reports to eBooks, one piece of content, strategic objectives

8. Deliver your message to the world. This can be done with interviews (both ways), media appearances, your blog, comments on other people's blogs (be strategic and ADD to the conversation), forums, record everything

9. Become an author. Writing a book gives you the ultimate credibility, and doesn't have to take very long to put together. I'll be going into greater detail on this I the next section.

10. Choose a charity to align yourself with, based on your personal experiences and beliefs. The organization I talk about the most is Rotary. This is an international service organization helping people in a variety of ways. The work I do with Rotary resonates with my target audience, no matter where in the world they live.

11. Use the Power of Compression - compression = speed + power, power of stacking, External Independent Confirmation, gives you momentum

12. Leverage Your Position - leapfrog your way to the top, create your own products, hold your own workshops, speaking engagements

## Idea Generation

So, where do you get your ideas for your online business? Ideas can come from most anyplace, so you must get into the habit of recording them. I keep a small notebook in my purse at all times, as well as one in my car, another one in my carry-on bag when I travel, and one in both of my home offices. I write down everything that comes to me, along with one or two descriptive sentences, so that I can look back at these ideas later on and take action on them.

I might be talking to someone at a meeting, emailing with a student, reading a book, watching a movie, thinking about what I'm going to prepare for dinner, or any of a dozen other scenarios when an idea for a new product or blog post or course strikes me. Most recently I was thinking about how to make sure people found what they were looking for when they misspelled the link to one of my sites. That's how the idea for my *cPanel Profits* course was born. Train yourself to record your thoughts and ideas so you'll be able to recognize and use the great ones to build your business.

Remember that entrepreneurs are not born; they are created when someone acknowledge that they want and need to harness your ideas into tangible resources that will serve other people. You can become a successful entrepreneur by learning as much as possible and setting your mind to achieving your goals.

## It All Begins With Your Blog

I am well know for saying that your blog is your 'Home on the Internet'. By this I am referring to your hosted Wordpress blog, where you own the site and the content and can freely share your thoughts and ideas with your readers. When set up and maintained regularly, your blog can be an additional income stream in your online business.

So just how do you monetize your blog? The step between creating and setting up your blog and earning an income from it is essentially the process we call "monetization." Monetization is the process that most online entrepreneurs seek to master. Achieving that goal takes some effort and dedication, but it really is not that difficult especially when working with a blog.

## Relationship Marketing

What makes a blog uniquely suited as a platform for monetization is its ability to facilitate the production of fresh, interactive content for readers. That's a formula for repeat visitors which is the goal of any business. Repeat visitors reflect well upon a blog publisher as it means that the content being created is meeting a need. As a smart business owner it would serve you well to take note of that need in your market and determine if there are not only content solutions but product or service solutions that you can sell to your audience to improve their satisfaction levels even further.

To illustrate, imagine if your local supermarket published a daily blog that offered daily updates on meat and dairy discounted specials along with new and unique freshly baked items ready for pick up that day. You might very well check that website every morning to confirm your meal plan for the day and to take advantage of any discounted food savings available.

If updated regularly with the kind of information shoppers appreciate, before long that supermarket website would attract quite a crowd of loyal readers, likely comprised of the people in your neighborhood who like shopping at that supermarket and who appreciate getting a heads up on specials that they can readily access any time of the day through their various computer devices (mobile and desktop).

The kind of relationship that can be developed by intuitive and committed blog publishers with and an intended audience is a unique relationship that is the basic requisite for building a lasting and profitable monetization strategy for your blog.

## Affiliate Marketing On Your Blog

Once you have decided to earn some substantial income with your blog you are to be congratulated on your positive thinking and entrepreneurial spirit. I'm going to explain how to take action on this idea right away and turn it into reality, as I and thousands of others are doing every day. The step between setting up and posting to your blog and earning an income from it is essentially the process that is referred to as "*monetization*". Monetization is the process that most entrepreneurs, online businesses, and marketers seek to master. Achieving that goal takes some effort and dedication, but it really is not that difficult, especially when working with a blog.

What makes your blog uniquely suited as a platform for monetization is its ability to facilitate the production of fresh, interactive content for your readers on a regular basis. That's a winning formula for repeat visitors to your site, which is the goal of any online business. Repeat visitors reflect well upon a blog publisher as it means that the content being created is meeting a specific need. As a savvy entrepreneur it would serve you well to take note of that specific need in your market and determine if there are not only content solutions, but also affiliate product and service solutions, that you can recommend to your audience to improve their satisfaction levels even further.

Your blog is an excellent platform for earning income as an affiliate marketer. As a 'Super Affiliate', where I now earn five figures a month, every month, from promoting other people's products and services, I feel uniquely qualified in sharing my experiences with you here. I'll be completely honest as I tell you what works, what does not work, and which strategies and methods I use personally on my two main blogs:

HugeProfitsTinyList.com
ConnieRagenGreen.com

# Your Monetization Strategy

From preparing and publishing content in the form of blog posts, reviews, and reports to determining ways to attract new visitors and engage old ones, you have several opportunities to sell to your audience in ways that can complement the information being shared. Selling doesn't have to be unpleasant or distasteful. With your blog you have an opportunity to integrate marketing and selling activities seamlessly into the overall content marketing strategy used on your site. If you're running a business to make a profit everything you do should support that goal or you won't be in business for long.

Affiliate marketing works perfectly in that you will only be recommending what you have purchased, used, and benefitted from. I refer to this as 'recommending what you love', and I've build an extremely profitable business based on this premise. I've also written a book on this topic and am considered an expert in the area of affiliate marketing. More information about my book can be found at the end of this report in the 'Resources' section.

Sometimes we can get so caught up in the work of building a relationship with the people in our audience so that we begin to shy away from and forget about our job of promoting and recommending services and products on our blogs. I teach that your blog is your 'Home on the Internet'. Ultimately your blog is your business and you've always got to keep that reality top of mind and stay focused on this idea regularly.

To help you to focus on strategies that will keep you on target with respect to serving the needs of your audience and the fulfilling the goals of your business plan, check your blog marketing activities against the following three guiding questions for business blogs:

Are the activities you are adopting to monetize your blog helping you to:

- Interact with your target audience to get to know them better
- Build a relationship with them as a trusted advisor who cares
- Educate them about how what you recommend will be helpful with the goals they wish to achieve

By asking the simple questions above you can help to ensure that in the midst of addressing multiple priorities and tasks in your business and on your blog that you do not overlook key opportunities and strengths of a successful blog and the feedback and needs of your own target audience.

## Choosing a Monetization Strategy

You have a number of options you can take to increase the profitability of your blog but to increase your chances of success you should create a strategy that clarifies:

1. Your revenue goals – how much do you want and need to earn?
2. The needs of your target market – which strategies will work best to meet their needs?
3. Time management – will you be willing to devote the necessary time to implement what you decide to do?

Once you've considered your needs and available resource you are then ready to determine how best to monetize your blog to suit your own needs and goals. Let's talk about some of these options.

## Monetization Methods

There are many ways to monetize your blog as an affiliate, including direct ad sales; Google AdSense; advertising networks; sponsored posts; and sponsored reviews. However, I do not recommend that you use any of these I have listed, especially in the beginning of your online marketing career. Instead, take the time to learn more about and implement what I will now share with you. These methods work, and you will find that they work extremely well if you implement them on your own blog.

There are five primary ways that I recommend you use to earn affiliate income from your blog. The first is from your posts, where you discuss a topic specific to your niche and include a reference to an appropriate affiliate product that makes sense. Secondly, you will want to add affiliate banners in the side bar of your blog. Then, you may wish to write affiliate product reviews as posts on your blog. Next, you can write short reports that focus on a particular topic or theme and include these as downloadable reports directly from the main page of your blog. Finally, include an opt in form in a prominent position on the upper right-hand side of your blog to build a list that you can continue to stay connected with and market to over time.

I use all five of these marketing strategies on each of my two main blogs, and will go into greater detail on each of them here.

### #1 - Your Posts

Writing blog posts may sound like a tedious and time-consuming endeavor, but suffice it to say that every moment you spend on this will be helpful to building your online empire.

I think of my posts as the first stop in turning my thoughts and ideas into something tangible – writing. As I discuss my topic in both general and specific ways, it makes sense for me to include affiliate links to products and services that will benefit my readers. You can do the same thing.

Another strategy I have been using for a few years now is to purchase a domain name and forward it to one of my posts. The post then shows up on its own page, allowing me to create an eCourse from that post. I recommend many affiliate products throughout, and that brings me additional income for years to come. An example of how I do this is at:

http://ProductivityChallengeOnline.com

In the beginning it will feel like it takes forever to write your blog posts. All of us feel that way, I believe. I used to agonize over what to write, and then spend hours doing the writing. Over time it all became much easier, and now I think of an idea and write it very quickly. Just remember that your journey begins with the first step, so take that step today and just start writing. Once you find your voice it will be a joy to share your thoughts and ideas on your niche topic with the people who are coming to you as their trusted advisor.

## #2 - Affiliate Banners

I have banners on the right-hand sidebar of both of my main sites, and for a very good reason – they work! Take a look again at my two main blogs:

http://HugeProfitsTinyList.com

http://ConnieRagenGreen.com

Do you see the sidebar on the right? Just below my opt in box I have a few affiliate banners. The people I am an affiliate for provide these banners, so all I need to do is copy and paste them into the 'widgets' that are a part of Wordpress.

Look to see which affiliate programs you are a part of offer banners for you to use on your blog.

## #3 - Affiliate Product Reviews

One of the most common ways for bloggers and other website publishers to earn an income online is through affiliate sales achieved through "affiliate marketing" on a blog/website. Before we explore the potential for generating income through affiliate product reviews, let's first be clear on the definition of an affiliate marketer.

If you receive payment in return for promoting through your own blog/website a product or service that is created and produced by someone else, you are an affiliate marketer. You don't produce or deliver the product or service being sold and you're not involved in processing the sale, but you are associated with the product/service because you've agreed to promote it on your website in return for a fee or commission based on sales related to your promotion. That makes you an "affiliate" for that product or service and the actions you initiate on your blog to promote it are essentially marketing tactics. Taken all together these actions qualify you as an affiliate marketer.

One of the main ways you can monetize your blog is by writing reviews for products and services that you represent as an affiliate. In these reviews you would include your personalized links to the product or service you're recommending. Anyone clicking that link would be taken to an information page or shopping cart page located on the affiliate product/service owner's website.

How you are compensated will be based on the number of leads or "clicks" you generate through your post or on the number of actual sales resulting from readers on your site who click on your affiliate link and eventually purchase the product or service.

The whole process of matching up the affiliate with the lead or sales generated is an automated one that is handled by various types of software that can be used by the affiliate product/service owner. That software creates unique links that are shared with affiliates when they sign up to be an affiliate marketer.

When bloggers insert a link to an affiliate product in a post they are writing, they will use the affiliate link assigned to them to ensure that they are appropriately credited when leads or sales are generated through that link.

What you sell and how much you get paid will depend on your preferences, the terms of the affiliate program and even what you are able to negotiate with the affiliate product/service owner based on the potential of your site to generate high sales.

For anyone who has ever hated the idea of face-to-face selling but loved the idea of generating an income based on lucrative sales commissions, affiliate sales may be just the ticket for you. If you believe in the product/service you are recommending and can write about it in a way that appeals to your target market, you'll end up selling in a way that is painless and profitable!

Super affiliates, such as myself, are known to make well into the six-figure range based on their target market, the volume of website traffic they are able to attract and their skill at promoting various products or services through well-written content. All of this comes in time, so the important thing is to just get started.

Here again, as mentioned earlier, the FTC requires full disclosure when publishing paid content. Affiliate product reviews are considered paid content since you expect to be compensated for leads and/or sales resulting from your blog post. Add your disclosure to your blog in a prominent position that can easily be seen by visitors to your site.

## #4 - Short Reports

I love short reports! These continue to earn me lots of money and they are simple to put together. If you go to one of my main sites – http://ConnieRagenGreen.com – you will see 'Short Reports' in my tool bar. When you hover over that, you will see that I currently have seven different reports that I am offering at no cost or obligation.

These reports are a combination of my own writing, a compilation of blog posts and articles I have previously written, PLR (private label rights) content I have access to, and content written together with a partner.

Be sure to have a call to action at the end of your report, and a footer that takes readers back to a site where they can learn more about you and the product or service you are recommending. In the Resources section at the end of this report there is a link to a course that will teach you everything you need to know about writing short reports.

## #5 - Building a List

The ultimate goal for earning income as an affiliate marketer is for you to take your visitors away from your site and on to your list. This is the concept of moving people away from the 'Big Playground' of social media and the Internet in general and moving them over to 'Your House' where you make the rules and control the ball. It's a simple analogy that works well for online entrepreneurs.

Make sure to have an opt in box on your blog, on the right-hand side and above the fold, just the way I have on my two main blogs. Offer a free giveaway that will compel visitors to sign up for your list, and then stay connected with them for as long as they are a subscriber by sending out autoresponder and broadcast emails. I send seven to ten emails a week, and have done this successfully for more than five years now.

The gold is in the list and the follow up, as well as the relationship you build with your subscribers over time.

# Next Steps

One of the most common reasons that well-intentioned bloggers never really earn the full-time income they dream of isn't because of competition, cost or difficulty. The reason profitable blogging escapes many is that they don't follow through on the kinds of strategies articulated in this monetization guide.

Here are some success steps that I believe you will find helpful:

Believe that you can do this. My motto has always been 'If I can do it, you can do it'. I have no special talents or skills. I even type with two fingers to this day!

Invest time and money into your education with books, trainings, and live events. You've already done this with everything you have purchased up to this point, so you must know how important this is in order to become more than you are today.

Refuse to give up! I always say that any sane person would have give up during the first few months, but I persevered and kept moving forward. Be persistent in your quest for success as an online entrepreneur.

Know that I am here for you. Connect with me to ask your questions and share what you are working on. One way to do this is through attending my bi-monthly open teleseminar at: http://AskConnieAnything.com

Instead of insisting that everything be in place perfectly before you begin, start today by writing a post and publishing it on your blog. Include an affiliate link that is appropriate and relevant to the subject you are writing on. You can do this!

## Becoming An Author

Becoming an author is the natural progression of being a successful online entrepreneur and is included as one of the twelve success steps I mentioned earlier. I've read that more than eighty percent of the population of the western world would like to write a book, yet fewer than one percent ever turn their dream into reality. This is my ninth book, so if you look at the statistics the likelihood of me, or anyone achieving this goal seems infinitesimal. Yet, I personally know more than a hundred people who have penned at least one book. How is this possible?

I have found that entrepreneurs move quickly past the naysayers and those who will still be talking about writing their book years from now. They are action takers who will find out what needs to be done and then do it, rather than spending countless hours analyzing the different ways to accomplish their goals, the pros and cons of doing something in a specific way, and so forth. If you are to be successful in this lifestyle, get used to moving forward and implementing your ideas quickly.

Now, let's get back to your becoming a published author. There are many ways to accomplish this goal, but for the purposes of establishing yourself as a credible expert it's best to do as I have done since self-publishing my first book in 2010. Your process will evolve over time, but the basic premise is that you have unique information and experiences that need to be shared with others, and the best way to do this is through the writing and publishing of it in book format.

# Your Internet Lifestyle Plan

Living the Internet lifestyle is simple, but it won't be easy without a plan. If you are to be successful as an online entrepreneur living the Internet lifestyle then you must start out with a step by step plan to get your business off the ground. My suggestion is that you go through each of these steps and then go back and reread the previous sections of this book where I have gone into much greater detail.

Here are the initial ten steps:

1. Choose a niche
2. Purchase hosting and a domain name
3. Install a Wordpress blog
4. Create a short report to use as your free giveaway
5. Set up an autoresponder sequence
6. Start blogging regularly
7. Become active on social media
8. Find a mentor
9. Choose three or four products to recommend as an affiliate

10. Spend some time every day thinking about and focusing upon the goals you wish to achieve

You will feel so proud of yourself once you implement these steps, knowing you are on your way to a lifestyle you can make your own to suit your needs and desires. I have oversimplified these steps, but I can assure you that these skills, like everything in business, are learnable ones that you or anyone for that matter can easily master.

The resources are readily available for you to get started, either through my earlier books, or by going to YouTube or Google and typing in exactly what you need. I have learned so many things through these two mega sites, some of which I have turned into products and courses to share with others in a more detailed way.

Here are some more advanced steps you will take as soon as you have the first ten steps in place.

1. Create systems so that many parts of your business will run on autopilot. This includes your autoresponder emails, social media, and syndication of your writing.

2. Start putting together a team of trusted colleagues who will be there for you. This would include help with technology, marketing, copywriting, and anything else you feel you might struggle with as you get started.

3. Choose someone from your team to act as a Project Manager for everything you want to do. If you can find someone who has worked as an executive assistant in the past, snap them up and add them to your team.

4. Enlist the services of a VA (virtual assistant) who can do the clerical aspects of this business for you. This will save you lots of time, energy, and frustration.

5. Set up a schedule and marketing calendar for everything you do in your business. Staying focused and organized makes it all more fun and productive.

This is how the biggest names on the Internet are running their businesses, so you might as well start doing the same thing from the very beginning.

# Section Four

# Thinking BIGGER

*'Great minds discuss ideas;*
*average minds discuss events;*
*small minds discuss people.'*
*Eleanor Roosevelt*

I will now share with you some things I have learned, based on my experience as an online entrepreneur since 2006. Once you have enough money to pay all of your bills comfortably each month, as well as having enough money to help members of your family, to travel, and to enjoy some of the finer things in life, you will begin to expand your thinking in a new and wonderful way. Here is where I want to encourage you to think bigger than you ever have before and have ever even thought possible.

One of my dreams was to travel; now I travel internationally to speak at seminars and conferences, as well as to do charity work. Any vacations I choose to take with family and friends will always be more memorable because I look for a way to help others while I am there. Another dream I had was to spend more time at the beach to breathe in the fresh ocean air; I now have a home that overlooks the ocean. I dreamed of having enough money to pay all of my financial obligations with grace and ease; now I look for additional tax deductions!

Your life can and will change quite dramatically if you are willing to build your business from the ground up, following the steps I am laying out in this book. That's why I emphasize the quote I presented at the beginning of this book:

*'Be willing to do what others will not for a year;*
*Be able to live the way others cannot, forever.'*

What do you want in your life? That becomes the question you must acknowledge and address every day. It's the people in your life who matter, and having the time and financial resources to make life better for others around you is a worthwhile goal.

I'm all about helping others to reach their full potential. As a child you may have heard your teacher say something like this to your parents in regards to your academic progress. Teachers will often say that a child is not reaching their full potential because they are daydreaming and not participating with the other students. I believe just the opposite; daydreaming is required in order for you to reach your potential in life. You must also make some big changes, to your strategy, to your life story, and to your thinking.

Change your strategy as you move forward. Find someone doing what you want to do and do more of what they are doing. Allow me to explain further.

When I got started back in 2006 there was no social media, so it was difficult to connect with the people who were already successful with having a business on the Internet. That meant I had to search for them online, and when I found someone whose ideas resonated with me I quickly joined their list. My goal was to watch what they were doing and to emulate it, using my own voice and style. I'm still friends with some of these people today – Marlon Sanders, Kathleen Gage, and others.

Find a few people who are doing what you'd like to be doing and learn from the steps they take each day in their business. Take classes from them, ask questions, and implement what you learn as quickly as you can.

Change your story. This goes back to the self-talk I discussed early on in this book. If you're a complainer, knock it off. Think about and reframe your life experiences into positive, useful ones that will serve you well for the rest of your life.

Change your mind as to your beliefs about being success, earning money, and living your day to day life. Think big and think positive and don't allow anyone or anything to get in your way.

A lot of times people have the most trouble just getting started on what they want in regards to their goals and dreams. It's all about changing your point of attraction to what you want in your life.

You may have heard about something called 'set point' in regards to weight loss. It's the point where your body gets stuck and does not want to release any excess weight. You must make drastic changes to both your food intake and exercise routine in order to see any results.

There's a 'set point' for your income as well. I went through this for twenty years as a teacher and a real estate appraiser. Any time I would earn some extra money it wasn't long before I'd have a setback of some type that took me right back to my previous earnings level. Some unexpected expense would come up, or my time would be mismanaged, and the extra money would be gone in a flash.

It wasn't until I shook everything up by starting my online business and finding the proper training that I was able to break through my income 'set point'. Does this explanation of set point make any sense when you think about your own experiences?

I can relate to and understand this because I used to be the same way. I know what it feels like to be stuck and not sure which way to turn.

It wasn't until I was about to turn fifty years old, in over my head with debt, at a job I was no longer passionate about and not sure what my next move would be that the light switch was turned on for me. It all started when I made the conscious decision to find a way to change my life forever. You can do the exact same thing in a way that will work for the lifestyle you want to achieve.

Working online continues to be a rewarding way to earn a living while teaching and connecting with others.

# Productivity

*"Perhaps the very best question that you can memorize and repeat, over and over, is, "what is the most valuable use of my time right now?"*
*Brian Tracy*

The key to success in anything in life, whether it's in enjoying the Internet marketing lifestyle or anything else your heart desires, is to stay focused, organized, and diligent in your pursuit of your goal. Productivity is crucial, and here is an excerpt of a conversation I had with Geoff Hoff, my co-author on two of my books, on this topic.

**Geoff:** Connie, earlier in the book, you talked about how you lived paycheck-to-paycheck when you were a teacher, and how your money usually ran out before the next paycheck, but that there was nothing you could do about that, since you were already doing everything you could. How has your idea of productivity evolved since then?

Living the Internet Lifestyle

**Connie:** I haven't thought about those days for quite a long time, Geoff, but I'm glad you've brought it up here. During those years, when I was struggling to balance my life in regards to family, health, finances, and two careers, it seemed like I was spinning my wheels and not being very productive in any of these areas.

It was all I could do each day to wade through the tasks I needed to complete in order to leave my house before six in the morning, do everything that had to be done in my classroom once I arrived at my school, go on to my real estate appointments after school, and then get back home and deal with my family before going to sleep in anticipation of doing it all again the following day. It was exhausting, to say the least.

The reality was that my productivity was at a very high level because I was managing my time so well. It just didn't feel that way because I wanted so much to be doing something else in my life at that time. I was caught up in what is referred to as the *momentum of mediocrity,* treading water but never quite making it out of the deep end of the pool.

The situation I am describing here happens to many of us, especially if we are doing tedious work that lacks the ability to spark our creative flow and doesn't pay very well. It's up to each of us to remove ourselves from the situation as quickly and as gracefully as possible to make room for whatever is to come in our life. I think of this as our unalienable right to seek our destiny.

This is the definition I share with my coaching students:

Proactive, Consistent Actions + Managed Time = Productivity

**Geoff:** It's fascinating to me that you say you were living "at a very high level of productivity and managing your time well" during this frantic time in your life. I know many of us have often found ourselves in circumstances where we are doing so much, feeling like we are using every available moment, and yet it seems nothing is progressing, nothing is moving forward at all.

When I was in college, I worked in the cafeteria for breakfast, lunch and dinner (and at special events such as when it was rented out for banquets), had a full load of classes, rehearsed in plays most evenings and found time to do my homework.

After college, I often held two jobs and still somehow found time to do "extracurricular" stuff like writing, working on plays, etc. (Of course, housework rarely seemed part of the bargain... ) Even with all of this, the feeling I have is that I wasn't being "productive". Looking at your example, I suspect it was because I didn't have any real plan or idea of where I was going, just a vague, general notion.

I think there are many who find themselves in this state, working very hard, but going pretty much nowhere. I'm reminded of the Red Queen in Alice in Wonderland who said, "Now, here, you see, it takes all the running you can do, to keep in the same place. If you want to get somewhere else, you must run at least twice as fast as that!" We feel like the only way to move forward is to do more, to "run twice as fast as that", and we feel like there isn't any more we can fit into the mix so we stay in the same place.

Given this, do you have any thoughts or suggestions about how we can, as you say, "remove ourselves from the situation as quickly and as gracefully as possible..."?

**Connie:** Removing yourself from the situation only applies to the tedious and mundane, and to situations where we have outgrown our usefulness, *not* to activities and tasks that we actually want to achieve. If that is the case, simply complete what you originally agreed to, like I did when I worked in the classroom through the end of the school year in June, and then move on quietly to the next phase of your life.

What I am hearing you describe, Geoff, fits in exactly with what I have come to call the '3 Ps of Super Productivity™'.

In order to be overly, or 'super' productive I believe that we must have at least one of the following active in what we are striving to achieve:

- Passion/Purpose – When we are passionate about an activity it will not only go quickly, it will also make our heart sing.
- Prime Time – Activities that are worked on during the hours that we are the most alert, focused, and engaged will always produce optimal results.
- Project-Based – Working on a project, whether it's by ourselves or with a team, brings out the best in all of us. This leads to a feeling of pride in a job well done.

As you are describing your job as a cafeteria worker during college, I am envisioning a team of strong young students, excited to be spending that time together each day. I imagine you, Geoff, as the one bringing humor and laughter to the work, creating contests to see who could fill the salt and pepper shakers the fastest and daring the others to set the tables in a unique way, perhaps with a salad fork replacing a soup spoon! I picture you as a leader who never saw that job as a menial one.

And knowing you as I do, I'll bet you were much more engaged during the dinner hour than earlier in the day, because your 'prime time' hours are much later in the evening.

When you talk about having time to write and participate in acting and producing plays, I hear and feel the passion coming through your words. That was your reward for doing the hard work during the days. Your work in the theatre is an excellent example of a 'project-based' activity, where you feed off the energy and excitement of your group members as you accomplish your goal of taking the play from inception to production.

It's the ideas that are generated during our best hours of each day (prime time), based on our passions and purpose for living our lives (passion/purpose), that lead to the fulfillment of our specific goals (project-based).

I have been known to write for hours on end when I am passionate about the project I am working on. A recent example of this was when legendary marketer Marlon Sanders asked me to create a bonus for his new product.

When I first started working on this bonus report it was during a week where I had so much to do and was feeling the stress from having been ill for several days and then traveling to another state to speak at an event. The result was that I chose a topic I was not passionate about, worked on it during non prime time hours when I was tired and at an energy 'low', and I was not discussing it with my Mastermind group, my entrepreneur friends, or my list, to get the team support I needed.

After speaking with Marlon (a true pioneer and genius in the online world) at length on the phone, he gave me an idea that inspired me to write a bonus report that I couldn't wait to begin working on. I was in the airport waiting for my flight home from the event where I had been speaking while he and I were on the phone, and I began taking notes before my flight ever took off.

I made some more notes during the flight, but waited until early the following morning (my prime time hours) to actually do the writing. Within about four hours I had written almost three thousand words on a topic I'm extremely passionate about, and then sent it off to him to add to his site as a bonus.

The next step was to share what I had accomplished with my community on social media, to my list, and with my circle of entrepreneur friends. I was floating on a cloud for the next couple of days because of what I had been able to accomplish after being inspired in that way.

Find inspiration anywhere you can, and then take action in a focused and productive way.

Geoff, I have seen you inspired by hearing certain speakers present at live events, by a book you were reading, and by conversations you've had with me or others. I have then witnessed you becoming super productive in a way that is achieved by few men, all because you have allowed yourself to expand in to these '3 Ps of Super Productivity™'.

So, let's expand our definition of Productivity from...

Proactive, Consistent Actions + Managed Time = Productivity

to...

Passionate, Purposeful, Project-based, Consistent Actions performed during our Prime Time = Super Productivity

Now that we have discussed this topic in some greater detail, I have a question for you:

Geoff, when you have been super productive in your business during this past couple of years, can you describe the feeling it gives you both during and after you have accomplished your goals?

**Geoff:** That's an interesting question and actually has several different answers. I'll start with the "after". I always have a sense of joy and contentment when I have accomplished something I set out to do. That's easy to answer and I suspect most people feel that way. However, when setting out to accomplish something, there are different experiences depending on what's going on.

When what I am attempting to accomplish is something I know I can do, that I know is fairly easy for me, whether I have a passion for it or not, the feeling I have when doing it is of an easy flow. I can easily slip into what people have often called "the zone" with such tasks and projects. What that feels like for me is that the rest of the world sort of disappears and all that is present is the task at hand. Often, when in this state, I have no sense of the passage of time and sort of "wake up" at the end being surprised that so much time has gone by.

That isn't how it always feels, of course. When the project is something I'm not sure I can accomplish, that I don't know if I have the skills or experience for, that enviable "zone" is far away. With those projects (and there have seemed a lot of them in the last few years) I am almost hyper-aware of the passage of time. I often feel like I'm working against time to get them done, as if I had some massive deadline, or, if you want to get mythological, the sword of Damocles hanging in the air above me, just waiting for the chance to drop.

Once these projects have been accomplished there is an added feeling of satisfaction, of course. I have an odd and slightly embarrassing habit of wanting to go back over them again and again, partly to admire them, but partly to actually see and acknowledge what I've accomplished. (This can be with projects as diverse as having written a piece that I didn't think I was knowledgeable enough or skilled enough to do, or something as mundane as a thorough house cleaning.) I will usually indulge myself in this habit for a short time, but then force myself to put this project aside and move on to the next one, or I would be fearful of transforming from Damocles into Narcissus, staring at my own reflection for eternity at the expense of everything else.

Then there are those times I'm working on something that starts out being one like the latter, where I am conscious of every twist and turn I must take and somehow in the process, fall into that "zone" where I wake up at the end having accomplished it almost automatically. These are rare, though.

One of the ways you mentioned to be more productive (and that we've touched upon earlier in this book) is to find those things that must be done but that we either aren't good at or don't necessarily like to do. What many of us don't quite realize until we've done it a few times is that delegating, or giving those tasks away to others, is a fairly high form of productivity. They are still being done, but we are freed up to do the things we love, are good at and that will make a bigger difference in our own lives, our businesses and the lives of those around us. As much as I am gratified by being able to accomplish new things, it might be better to forego that feeling, let someone else accomplish that task, and only keep for myself the things that I know I'm really good at.

You have had a much longer experience of both delegating and accomplishing things that move you forward and help you and your business grow. What is that experience like for you?

**Connie:** As has been the case many times throughout our relationship, I am finding myself once again needing to 'Google' for the references you make! This time it's to find out more about the "sword of Damocles". Ah, now I see what you mean.

I can totally relate to what you are saying in regards to getting into "the zone" and immersing myself in my work. I can become so engrossed that I am completely and totally oblivious to the sights and sounds around me. Dogs barking incessantly, phones ringing, and people talking remain outside of my realm of consciousness when I "zone out". This is a glorious state, and one that we can especially benefit from as entrepreneurs.

Also, I understand your habit of 'wanting to go back over them again and again, partly to admire them, but partly to actually see and acknowledge what I've accomplished' when it comes to completing a task you have undertaken and achieved. Perhaps this is our attempt to recreate the experience so that it becomes deeply ingrained in our subconscious mind.

It's so interesting how we create these situations for ourselves where we are racing the clock, looking over our shoulder, and forcing ourselves to complete a certain task by a specific date and time. I see this as our subconscious mind's way of pulling us back into the time in our past where we had a boss or a supervisor who had so much say over our day to day life.

While I was teaching it was the school's principal who imposed these walls around my creativity. While working in real estate it was the client or the lender urging me forward while they cracked the whip at my heels. Actually, truth be told, the way I was feeling during these years of my life was simply me allowing others to make me feel a certain way. Once I let go of the anger surrounding my relationships with these authority figures in my working life, I was able to reframe it as them urging me to do specific tasks in a specific way in order to reach my full potential.

I visualized the principal, Mrs. Kravitz, as a wise and thoughtful soul who had my best interest at heart. My reframe included her always looking out for me by pushing me, ever so gently at first and then in a more forceful manner to achieve more in my career as an educator. This was quite a stretch from how I felt for many years when I was allowing her to upset me almost every day for the six years I worked at that particular school.

When I was first working online and building my business I was embarrassed to admit the fact that I had worked for others until the age of fifty. But the online world is primarily non-judgmental, so I finally opened up and discussed my work history with the people who were attracted to learning from me. I shared how I felt as an employee for the public school district and as an independent contractor during my years as a real estate broker and appraiser, and how it all changed once I left that life behind and became the mistress of my domain.

As an entrepreneur we are freed of this bondage and must remind ourselves regularly of this freedom. My focus each day is to spend time doing what I love, which is writing, reading, learning, and creating, and then delegating and outsourcing everything else to people who are far more skilled than I am. These activities include setting up websites, rewriting private label rights content, spending time on the social media sites, and setting up my teleseminars, webinars, podcasts, and interviews.

I have long believed that we must not engage in the activities we do not truly enjoy because we are then taking that away from the person who does. Imagine someone taking on the tasks they dislike or have difficulty with, when these are ones you love to do, and not giving you the opportunity to do it for them? It would not feel right for either of you. Yet that's exactly what we are doing when we spend our precious time doing things that do not suit us.

Over time your preferences will change, so that something you once loved to do (in my case it was bookkeeping and preparing my income taxes) becomes something you have no desire to ever do again (the people who now handle this for me are computational wizards who make it all seem like child's play from my perspective).

Finally, let's discuss the level of enthusiasm necessary to achieve maximum and optimal productivity. This will vary from project to project as you move forward with your business. If you are not as passionate about one project over another it does not in any way diminish what you accomplish. For example, Geoff, as we finalize this last section of this book on time management strategies for entrepreneurs, we are not quite as excited and enthusiastic as we were when we wrote the original manuscript several months ago. This only means that we are both deeply involved with other projects at this time and is in no way a reflection on our commitment to excellence with this final addition to the book.

However, there is a direct correlation between your speed of implementation and your income, so do not allow anyone or anything to get in your way when you have a new idea.

Geoff, say something about the amount of time it now takes for you to go from creative thinking and initial idea to completed project when it comes to one of your digital information products or online courses.

**Geoff:** I think that question goes right to the heart of why some people are more productive than others. There are people who, as soon as an idea occurs to them, they put things into place to make that idea happen. Then there are those who ponder the idea, discount the idea, set the idea aside, or even think, "yes, that's a good one", then either wait for inspiration as to how to do it, or simply don't start because they don't immediately know how to accomplish it.

I think the ability to immediately put things into practice is one that can be learned. I've seen and heard about people who do it all the time, but it isn't necessarily an innate gift. It's one which must be developed. For me, there are ideas I get that seem grand ones, but also seem like they will take me off the path to what it is that I want to accomplish in the bigger scheme of things. It doesn't take a long time for me to determine if something will take me toward that or away from that. If it will take me away, I put it aside. If it seems it will take me toward my ultimate goal, I'll want to start jotting down ideas about it right away and move forward as quickly as possible.

However, often, I will come up with a good idea, jot notes, begin planning, and then set it aside for any of a number of reasons. When I do this, rekindling it can be difficult. This is where working with other people can become invaluable. When you have told someone you are going to create something and they are waiting for it, even if the initial passion or purpose has begun to face, that promise, that desire on another person's part can be something to anchor to, something you can attach yourself to in order to put into place what needs to be there to get the project done.

As an example, I have a book that I've been working on for quite some time. It's about the myths that artists cling to that keep them from producing their art. I have most, if not all, of the content done, but the shape of it was wrong, somehow. It wasn't coming together at all. But I have an accountability partner and I'd told her that I was working on it and wanted to get a draft of it done by a certain time. When I realized that I needed to go back and rework it, it would have been very easy to just let it go. However, her commitment to me getting it done re-infects me and this project is now taking shape rather nicely.

What is your experience of that, the time from the creative idea, through the planning to the completed project?

**Connie:** I'll get to my answer to that question, but first I'll say that I agree completely with you that in order to be optimally, or 'super' productive we must choose projects that will move us closer to our 'Big Picture' goals. I teach that for every action you take throughout your day, whether it is related to our business, our health, our relationships, or to something else we must always ask the question "Will this action move me closer to or further away from my goal?" we must continue doing what will move us closer and immediately cease all actions that are moving us further away. Delegating and outsourcing can be invaluable here.

It is also true that being able to take immediate action on an idea is a learnable skill. Practice makes perfect with this, so look for opportunities to stretch yourself in this area.

It was when I was first working with a Mentor and his Mastermind group five years ago that I encountered the problem of not being able to implement new ideas immediately. We would brainstorm ideas for each other for many hours over a three day period in the group meetings, and then each member received an mp3 recording of their session to listen to later on. This was convenient for everyone, as it's difficult to take notes while you're front and center and the group is hurling ideas at you at the speed of sound!

The problem was that I would listen to the replay a week or so later, take a few notes on what they had suggested, and then go about my daily routine. If they had recommended something small, like changing my picture on a profile page or changing a headline on a sales letter I would do that right away. The deeper, more detailed changes would take me weeks, or even months, and sometimes I would not take action on them at all. It was as if I was paralyzed into inaction. Looking back, I'm not sure what was stopping me from taking immediate action, but perhaps it was my lack of confidence in my abilities or a lack of being totally committed to my business as an online entrepreneur. In any case, I lost much time due to this and

I have to take 100% responsibility for the outcome during that period of time.

I then made it my goal to implement what I had learned and had been told by people I trusted, within seven days. This wasn't easy, but running a successful business requires that you stretch outside of your comfort zone on a daily basis.

The results were quite impressive; each time I took action I could see the fruits of my labor within days or weeks. Also, as I became more skilled in working faster, smarter, and more diligently, my mind was opened to more possibilities.

You may have heard a saying that goes something like 'fail fast, fail often, and fail forward'. This is what I strive to achieve every day in my business, as well as in my personal life. This is not an audition, this is real life and it's time for our most effective performance each and every day. We don't need to ask permission or give a thought to what anyone else would think. It's time for massive action!

Geoff, I'd like to wax philosophical now. We in the Western world tend to be 'in our heads' a lot, and perhaps that is part of the reason we do not accomplish our goals in a straightforward way as many Eastern cultures seem to be able to do. How do you get inspired to be productive, and how can you and I inspire others to do the same?

**Geoff:** What a wonderful question. I don't often talk about that part of things because it can scare people away, but I believe we are 100% responsible for our own inspiration. We think of it as some muse, something separate from us, whispering in our ear or prodding us to do something, but it is actually our subconscious mind, which has been churning and mixing all the information we have fed it, feeding that information back to us in new and exciting ways.

There are lots of different ways to be responsible for our own inspiration, and I could go on about it for hundreds of pages (in fact, I have gone on about it for hundreds of pages in other forums than this) but there are very practical things we can do every day to jump-start ourselves, to focus in so we can accomplish great things.

Sometimes, all it takes is focus, but most of us in the Western world don't quite know how to direct our own focus. One of the many exercises I like to do (and I call it an "exercise" on purpose. It may seem like I'm advocating meditation, and, although meditation can be very powerful, this is not that. It is something far less esoteric and far more grounded in practical reality) is to start the day with working my imagination. How I structure it is to open a blank document on the computer, take a brief moment to get an idea, then start typing the details of some wonderful future.

I fill in details for three or four paragraphs, never stopping to edit, never worrying about if any of it is possible. It's just a dream, but it's a focused one. I usually find myself beginning to smile a few sentences in, however. Once I'm done, I sit for a very brief moment, "recalling" that future that I just made up, then see what's on the schedule and get to work.

This exercise does several things. It is extremely pleasant, for one, and so it is easy to do. It also gets our mind really focused. Once we are in a focused state, it's very easy to continue to focus on the next task and the next. This way, our day starts both pleasantly and with direction.

If that one doesn't appeal to you, there are many audios out there that are designed to help you focus. I'm not talking about hypnosis or, again, meditation, I'm simply talking about things that bring the mind in from the frantic wandering we are used to in our busy lives. (I've even created some of these audios myself and people seem to respond very well to them.) Something that takes ten minutes or less can change our entire day.

You may have noticed that I keep insisting it isn't meditation. Meditation can be, as I said, a very powerful thing and science has shown us that it can even alter our thought patterns. However, meditation has connotations of magic. Also, true meditation, like the Yogis can do, takes years to perfect and we in the Western world simply don't have those years. It also takes a long time to meditate and we usually don't have several hours at the start of the day to give over to that. Having something quick simple to use is all we really need.

So when I find myself "uninspired" to move forward (and, yes, it still happens to me), I find one of the many exercises I've found or created over the years to assist me to get focused and present to what needs to be done, spend five or ten minutes with that, then get to work.

(In our book, "The Inner Game of Internet Marketing", I go into greater detail about several of these, by the way.)

Connie, I also know that you have techniques that you use that may not seem at first glance to be part of "time management" or "productivity" but that help you get done what you need to do. Can you elaborate on any of them?

**Connie:** I'd be happy to, Geoff. Thank you for sharing your experiences with inspiration in regards to focus and productivity. And as far as pursuing a muse, I am reminded of the Albert Brooks film *The Muse* where a screenwriter seeks the help of a woman who appears to be a daughter of Zeus, in order to rekindle his writing career. But I digress.

I like to plan my life at least a quarter ahead. By this I mean that I keep a calendar of what I will be working on for the next three months or more. This includes personal goals, such as a trip or special event with family or friends, as well as business planning, which includes writing, product creation, affiliate promotions, and live events.

When someone asks me if I am available next month on the first Thursday at noon, it is easy to see if I already have something scheduled. This may seem like a simple thing, but I have much more free time when I schedule it all. Just this week I was able to attend the Cowboy Festival with some friends and neighbors, simply because I had added it to my calendar almost two months ago. Everything moves smoothly and effortlessly when you do this on a regular basis.

Earlier in the book, I talked about the 'rocks, pebbles, sand' where the philosophy professor poured ever smaller sizes of rocks and pebbles into a jar, finishing with sand to show that, if you focus first on the small stuff, there is no room for the stuff that is actually important.         You must take care of the important things, such as taking care of your health, finding the right people to share your life with, and building a profitable business with residual income if you are to get to a place in your life where you can put this model into place. I have many students who want to jump directly to the lifestyle without laying the foundation. This leads to disappointment, struggle, and disillusionment with the process I am describing here. Instead, focus on your 'rocks' each and every day.

Here are three steps to get started with moving ahead productively:

1. Commit to being productive every single day
2. Automate, templatize, and systemize everything you do more than once
3. Delegate and outsource what others can do better and faster than you can

Following these three steps will enable you to accomplish more in less time, will allow you to have more free time to spend as you like, and will raise your self-esteem as you gain a deeper appreciation of what you are doing in your business and personal life. One of my favorite quotes applies here:

"Do for a year what other won't, then live the rest of your life the way others can't".

Geoff, what else would you like to add?

**Geoff:** We've talked about productivity from several different viewpoints, now. The idea that we can be "productive" (i.e. very busy) and still not get anything done if we aren't focused on what we want to accomplish in our lives is very profound. We also touched a bit on how we can inspire ourselves (the only way we really *can* be inspired) to be more productive. These both point to the "inner" side of things. Then there are the practical steps to take to actually get things done. These are from the "outer" side of things. You need both, I think, to be really productive.

**Connie:** Yes, we must have both the 'inner' and the 'outer' to be balanced in our work and in our personal lives. I'd like to leave our readers with a short checklist for what they can put into place right now to be as productive as possible.

- Determine when your 'prime time' hours are and plan to work on your most important projects during that time each day. Because my best time is early in the morning, I guard that time by going to sleep by eleven or so most nights, and not scheduling anything else before nine or ten in the morning so I can leisurely work on my writing.

- Make sure to have what I refer to as 'quiet time' for at least thirty minutes once a day. Geoff talked about meditation, but this time can also be used to sit in quiet contemplation while you daydream about the solutions to your problems and the ways to achieve your goals.

- Find a Mentor or accountability partner to connect with at least twice a week. This person will help you to stay focused on what is important to you right now, over the next thirty days, and a year or two into the future.

- Stretch yourself every day. I'm not talking about physically, but that's an excellent idea as well to get the blood flowing to your brain. I'm referring to what is sometimes called 'thinking outside the box'.

I find that by challenging myself to learn and take action on something new on a regular basis, my life and my business have greatly benefitted. You will still feel the resistance, but knowing that everything you need to know is a learnable skill will make it possible for you to attain your goals. In recent times this has included learning some Finnish (not so easy!), line dancing, and cooking some of my favorite dishes.

- Write down exactly what you want to achieve, when you want to achieve it by, and when you actually do achieve it. This has now been scientifically proven to work. Simply by taking the time and making the effort to put your ideas and goals into writing changes the way your mind will synthesize it into more concrete terms.

We hope you have benefitted from this section of the book, and hope that you will now feel empowered to move forward productively. Best of success with everything you set out to achieve in your life and in your business. Let us know how we can be of service to you.

This is the end of the excerpt from our book on time management for entrepreneurs. I hope you have gleaned some insight from our conversation.

# Final Musings

Living the Internet lifestyle is a worthwhile endeavor on so many levels. Whether your goal is to travel more, retire a family member, spend more time with kids or grandkids, send the children in your life to private schools and enrichment programs, do more volunteering and charitable work, or achieve something else you have been dreaming of for years, becoming an online entrepreneur can help get you there more quickly than anything else I can think of.

Make the decision to get started right away, and then implement the steps and the strategies I have outlined in this book.

# Resources

My two main sites:

http://ConnieRagenGreen.com
http://HugeProfitsTinyList.com

Massive Productivity Timer:

http://MassiveProductivity.com

30 Day Productivity Challenge:

http://ProductivityChallengeOnline.com

Connect with me on Facebook:

http://www.Facebook.com/ConnieRagenGreen

# About the Author

Connie Ragen Green is an author, speaker, and online marketing strategist living in southern California. Teaching others how to get started online and create a profitable business is her passion and life's work.

Connie has now spoken on three continents and has students in more than twenty countries around the world.

When she is not travelling the world Connie spends her time volunteering and working with a variety of charitable organizations, including Rotary and Elk's, as well as helping out at the local Food Banks, afterschool programs, and the public library.

To learn more about living the Internet Lifestyle and becoming an online entrepreneur, be sure to visit:

**HowToLiveTheInternetLifestyle.com**

This site has been designed with you in mind, and will give you access to more information and resources as you begin your journey. It is my goal and intention to help you with this process in any way I possibly can.

Connie Ragen Green

www.ingramcontent.com/pod-product-compliance
Lightning Source LLC
LaVergne TN
LVHW022342060326
832902LV00022B/4184